An "Uncertaine Rumor" of Land

NEW THOUGHTS ON THE ENGLISH FOUNDING OF VIRGINIA'S EASTERN SHORE

JENEAN HALL

KWE PUBLISHING

Hall, Jenean. *An "Uncertaine Rumor" of Land*

Copyright © 2022 by Jenean Hall All rights reserved.

ISBNs: 978-0-9832660-1-3 (paperback), 978-0-9832660-2-0 (e-book)

Library of Congress Catalog Number: 2022910265

First Edition. All rights reserved. No portion of this book may be reproduced, stored in a retrieval system, or transmitted in any form or by any means - including by not limited to electronic, mechanical, digital, photocopy, recording, scanning, blogging or other - except for brief quotations in critical reviews, blogs, or articles, without the prior written permission of the publisher, KWE Publishing.

Jacket art and design ©

"Salt Water Ponds" (1884) by Mary Nimmo Moran. Public Domain (CCO), Smithsonian American Art Museum, Transfer from the National Museum of American History, Division of Graphic Arts, Smithsonian Institution.

Photograph by author - Page from the Colonial Court Orders, Northampton County, Virginia.

Maps prepared by Bill Nelson-Cartography

Cover design by Michelle Fairbanks | Fresh Design

Published by KWE Publishing: www.kwepub.com

This book is dedicated to
Janice H. Thompson,
my sister and friend

TABLE OF CONTENTS

Glossary   *vii*
A Few Notes Before You Begin   *xv*

English Boots and Boats   1
John Rolfe's Report   5
Captain George Yeardley   7
In the Wake of Captain Argall   13
Secretary John Pory   17
The Broadside   21
Pory's Opinion   25
Deputy Thomas Nuce   29
"The Burrough of Kiccowtan"   35
Also Happening in the Colony   39
John and Frances Blore   43
John Wilcocks   49
Thomas Savage, Dales Gift, and Lady Dale's People   55
Thomas Savage and George Yeardley   59
A Few Loose Threads   63
Final Thoughts   79

References   *81*
Index   *85*
Notes   *91*
Acknowledgments   *99*
About the Author   *103*

Glossary

Acchawmacke Creeke or River: Cherrystone Inlet today. In early records, this body of water and the land adjacent were called Cherrystones.

Against: As used in early geography descriptions, "against" (agaynst) usually meant "opposite" or "across from."

Ancient Planter: A planter who had been in the colony since before the time of Sir Thomas Dale and had stayed at least three years. The definition of an ancient adventurer and planter was given in the Virginia Company's 1618 instructions to George Yeardley. These instructions have come to be known as "the Great Charter."

Burgess: An elected representative to the General Assembly (later Grand Assembly) of colonial Virginia.

Calendar: In these early years, England still used the Julian or Old Style (OS) calendar in which the legal year began on March 25. England did not change to the Gregorian or New Style (NS) calendar until 1752; at that time, January 1 became New Year's Day. (To synchronize with the New Style, England dropped eleven days from its calendar in 1751.)

When a date is written with two years between January 1 and March 24, the first year is OS and the second year is NS. (For example, March 24, 1632/33, would be followed by March 25, 1633.)

Cherrystone: See Acchawmacke.

Commodities: Products that could be sold or purchased.

Council of State: Also called the council or the governor's council. The council was composed of men appointed by the king to assist the governor. Members of the council along with the governor formed the General Court and the Quarter Court. Men appointed to the council were usually wealthy and from prominent families. The council, along with the governor and burgesses, made up the General (Grand) Assembly.

Cousin-German: An early term for what today is called "first cousin."

Crop: "At this crop" meant the current crop. "At the next crop," meant the future crop. These terms were used in reference to tobacco payments.

Dales Gift: In 1614, Deputy Governor Thomas Dale sent Captain Samuel Argall and Thomas Savage, the interpreter, to the Eastern Shore Indians to negotiate for land and corn. The land they procured was at the lower end of the peninsula. It was named "Dale's Gift."

Demand: In early colonial days, this word seems to have had a different meaning than today. Its meaning seems to have been "to ask, expecting an answer."

Divident: An early term for dividend, or a person's designated portion of land. This word was used frequently in the early records, but seems to have disappeared from use today.

Fall of the leaf: Autumn. Sometimes seen as "leafefall."

Folio: (abbreviation: fol.) The leaves of the old court records were often numbered with the first page (always on the right) as folio 1. After turning the page, the page on the right (recto) was called "folio 2," whereas its opposing page on the left (verso) was called merely "page 2." Theoretically, this pattern would follow throughout the book: page 3, folio 3; page 4, folio 4, etc.

General (Grand) Assembly: In the Virginia Company's 1618 instructions, George Yeardley was told to form "a laudable form of Government by Magistracy and just laws for Happy guiding and governing of the people there inhabiting like as we have already done for the well ordering of our own courts here and of our officers and actions for the behoof of that Plantation..." Yeardley called together elected representatives from each plantation. Together with the governor and the council of state, these men formed the "General Assembly." (In February 1631/32, this legislative body changed its name to "Grand Assembly." Years later, it would change back again to the General Assembly.)

General Court: By 1660, this was the name given to Virginia's highest court. Earlier it was termed merely "Court" and "Quarter Court." It was composed of the governor and the Council of State. In the colony's early years, this court most often met in James City and sometimes in Elizabeth City.

Headright: In 1619, the Virginia Company, through its instructions to Governor Sir George Yeardley, introduced the headright system. In this plan, a certificate for fifty acres somewhere in Virginia was granted to each person who came to the colony. That person was counted as one headright. Each headright equaled fifty acres. The land didn't necessarily go to the person who arrived, it went to the person who paid the transportation costs. Ownership of a headright could be transferred or assigned to another person.

Hogshead: Tobacco was shipped in containers of a standard size. The hogshead is made to hold 64 gallons of liquid; whereas a barrel holds half that amount.

Hundred: The term "hundred" comes from the English practice of locating ten towns, or tithings (groups of ten families), at a settlement. (See Encyclopedia Virginia). In Virginia, the term was used for the investment plantations which were usually larger than an average, singleowner plantation.

James City: Jamestown. The Eastern Shore records refer to Jamestown as James City. In the early Virginia records, this is the name used most often.

Kequohtan, Kicotan, Kecoughtan: The name of the Indian village that the early settlers found at the site of today's independent city, Hampton, Virginia, on Hampton River. In the early days, the English called that river Southampton River.

Kine: Archaic word meaning "cows."

Magatty Bay: Originally, this was an area just south of today's Old Plantation Creek. It may be that Magatty Bay originally was what today may be thought of as the mouth of Old Plantation Creek, and Magatty Bay Pond, which was just south of that, is known today as Costin Pond. Magatty Bay became all of the area hugging the bayside, from the mouth of Old Plantation Creek down to today's Wise Point. Today, maps will show Magatty Bay (or a similar spelling) on the east side, seaside, of the Eastern Shore, but originally it was a bayside area.

Mainland: Virginia's Eastern Shore is separated from the main body of Virginia by the Chesapeake Bay. The mainland is the main portion of Virginia.

Mean: Poor, or shabby. If one came across the sentence, "He was a mean man," in the early records, its translation today would likely be, "He was a poor man."

Neck: An isthmus. On the Eastern Shore (a 75-mile long peninsula) the necks jut off from the sides, especially the bayside. Most of the necks are named, as in Savages, Old Town, Old Plantation, Wilsonia, Church, etc.

New Year's Day: March 25: see "Calendar."

Ordinary: An ordinary was the same as what we might call an "inn" or "tavern." This use of the word has an interesting history. Early courts, a collection of ordinaries (judges), met in private homes until someone of the community found the means to build a house where food and drink could be sold with a room large enough for a court meeting. When court wasn't in session, the house still was often called "the ordinary." Over time, the word "ordinary" was used less in relation to the court and more often in relation to its provision of drink, food, and lodging. Throughout the seventeenth century, Virginia's laws pertained to ordinaries as the word "tavern" was not yet in use.

Patent: Land that was acquired by certification of headrights. It was the king's grant.

Personal Adventure: A term used when a person paid his or her own passage to Virginia.

Plantation: In colonial Virginia, the earliest use of this term seems to have been in reference to the large corporations formed for growing tobacco. The term then could be used interchangeably with "settlement" and with "hundred." Later, the term seems to have been used for what today is called "a farm" and size wasn't a defining factor. (Later still, outside the scope of this book, the term came to mean a very large farming operation.)

Pounds, shillings, and pence: In colonial days, 1 pound = 20 shillings; 12 pence = 1 shilling. The amount 4 pounds, 2 shillings, 3 pence would be written as £4.2.3.

Pretend: In the early records, this term's meaning was to state or to affirm. It did not have the connotation of deception as it does today.

Privy Council: The king's highest-ranking council of advisors.

Quire: Choir. In a church, the choir is the area where the minister and singing choir sit. It usually is between the nave and the altar. The governor also sat in this area.

Salvages: A word often seen in the records to refer to Indians. It is an early spelling of the word "savages."

Seasoning: When colonists first arrived in Virginia, it took them several months (some said a year) to acclimate to being in the new world. The arduous journey often left them weak and made them more susceptible to diseases (many probably caused by new viruses and bacteria, of which they had no knowledge). The local leadership encouraged the Company to give these new people time to adjust before putting them to hard work. If they didn't have time "to season," they often died.

Servant: A servant was a person who was working off a debt, usually of the cost of their transportation to the colony. The contract for transportation was usually seven years, but it could vary by contract. At the end of the obligation, the servant received "freedom dues;" this was usually two sets of clothes and a quantity of corn. (See "Settlers/Colonists/Tenants/Planters")

Settlers/Colonists/Tenants/Planters: Early English men and women were referred to in the records by several descriptors. A planter was usually the owner or head of a farm. If you hadn't paid your own passage (and you weren't a family member), you were usually a servant under contract (indentured servant); however, most of the early Company contracts were tenant contracts that allowed a sharing of profits. Servants worked to pay an obligation, but did not share profits. EVERYONE was a colonist, having come to the Colony of Virginia. Everyone was also a settler, but that term often referred to the specific plantation (farm) where you lived. For example, you were a colonist in Virginia, helping to settle the Elizabeth City Plantation; therefore, you were an Elizabeth City settler. Colonist and settler are usually interchangeable words.

Shallop: A small, heavy workboat used for sailing and rowing in shallow waters. John Smith used a shallop to explore the Chesapeake.

Summer Sickness: In the early years of the colony, the mortality rate increased in the summer months. This seems to have been due to a lack of fresh drinking water and the increased exposure to contaminated waters because of the change in tidal flows. New colonists were particularly prone to sickness because of their weakened condition upon arrival, but even seasoned colonists were at risk in the presence of poor water and unsanitary conditions.

Tenant: A person who leased land. During Company times, the term was used in reference to people brought in to work for the Company for a share of the profits. Later, after the Company was dissolved, contracts for workers would be set up on an individual basis. (See Settlers, above.)

Tithes, tithable: A person who met the criterion to be taxed. The criterion changed over time. Most males who were of age to work were tithable. Before women were taxable, some men would hire women to work in the fields. The lawmakers got wise to that and changed the law to include women who worked in the fields.

Tun: A cask that holds 256 gallons. Also, it is a measure of capacity, equal to four hogsheads. This word is sometimes confused with the word "ton."

Virginia Company of London: In 1606, King James approved the charter of this joint-stock company for which shares were sold at £12 10s. The plan was to outfit ships, go to America, come back with riches, and pay dividends to the investors. Over its eighteen years, the Company was headed by two men: Treasurer Sir Thomas Smith and Treasurer Sir Edwin Sandys. By the time King Charles I dissolved the Company in 1624, it was into its fourth charter and was in debt for no less than £9000. (It is sometimes called the London Company.)

Werowance, werowans: The English often adopted Indian terms. This term became interchangeable with the word "king" in reference to Indian leaders. A werowance was the person of highest authority in a tribe.

A Few Notes Before You Begin

WHY THIS BOOK IS NEEDED

The last time I asked someone how Virginia's Eastern Shore came to be settled by the English, I was told that Thomas Savage came over from Jamestown and built a home near Cheriton, and the settlement grew from there. I'd heard a version of that story before. It's one of three basic stories often told about Eastern Shore English beginnings. The next most popular story is that Governor George Yeardley sent a group of Company tenants over to live and work on land off Cherrystone Inlet, and the settlement grew from there. The other story is that a saltworks was set up on Smith Island and the settlement grew from that. Each of these stories is exciting to imagine and each has a thread of truth, but none tells what really happened.

The shortfall of accuracy regarding the English founding of Virginia's Eastern Shore is not the sin of the storyteller; the storytellers are telling us what they've read, what they've heard, what they've come to know from the storytellers who came before. We've had a rich history of storytellers on Virginia's Eastern Shore. It's as if each decade gives us some new discovery, new pages deciphered, artifacts unearthed, stones turned, new theories to push us forward. The account you are about to read is merely another stone, another step. Someone will come behind me and add to the story, no doubt setting the record a little straighter. Until that time, here's what my research shows to be the story of how Virginia's Eastern Shore became an English settlement.

I'm going to start with a nutshell of the theory, and if you are interested in the context behind it, you have sixteen chapters to read. If you are an Eastern Shore or Virginia history "buff," I know you will want to read them. It's my hope that these chapters provide new light on some marvelous old stories.

IN A NUTSHELL

In 1620, John Blore harvested his fall crop and then left Falling Creek for the last time. Blore had given up this 100 acres because the place turned out to be a promising site for an iron works. The Virginia Company had promoted iron as the commodity it wanted most from the colony, and thus, Governor George Yeardley made it worth Blore's while to return the Falling Creek site to the Company. As compensation for his troubles, Blore received an additional forty acres elsewhere.

John and his bride, Frances, made their home on the south end of a broad neck on Virginia's Eastern Shore. To the west was the Chesapeake Bay; to the south and east was a creek that provided safe harbor for Blore's small shallop. The Blores had two servants, both were boys of working age. At least one other couple may have joined the Blores to work the ground on the 140-acre site.

Not long after the Blores seated their plantation, John Wilcocks leased a tract of land on the south shore of Ackomack River (today's Cherrystone Inlet), probably in the spring of 1621. Wilcocks hired several men who had been sent to Virginia as tenants to work Company land in Elizabeth City.

In the early fall of 1621, the colony's secretary, John Pory, crossed the bay in Governor Yeardley's ship at the behest of Yeardley who had fallen ill and couldn't go. Pory placed ten tenants on "the Secretary's Land," a 500-acre tract at the north shore of what today is known as Kings Creek. Pory wrote in his notes that this site was near Captain Wilcock's plantation, the better to support one another.

The Blores had been at work on their plantation almost a year and a half when word came that the mainland Virginia Indians had attacked the mainland colonists. The attack began at noon on March 22, 1621/22, three days before the new year.[1] By the end of that day, 357 men, women, and children—a quarter of the population—lay dead. The Eastern Shore native people did not participate in the attack, and thus, no English people living on the Shore at that time were harmed nor even knew the attack had happened. Let me repeat: the Eastern Shore Indians did not participate in this attack. This is a fact that non-Eastern Shore people often miss.

Three months later, Governor Wyatt (who had been in office only four months at the time of the attack) commissioned the former governor, Sir George Yeardley, to go into the bay and find a habitable place for 300 to 400 colonists. Yeardley engaged Thomas Savage to go with him on this mission, because—to place that many colonists—the blessing of the local Indians would be necessary. Thomas Savage was the colony's most skilled interpreter. Through his trade expeditions, he had developed a friendship with the Eastern Shore werowance; in fact, the werowance referred to Savage as "my son."

Yeardley took the opportunity of this expedition to carry Lady Elizabeth Dale's cattle and cattlemen to safety on the lower Eastern Shore. He no doubt conferred with Blore and Captain Wilcocks for their opinions about the best place for a settlement. Afterward, Yeardley and Savage met with the werowance, a man whom the Englishmen called "the Laughing King." The werowance's compassion for the Englishmen's plight was extraordinary. Not only did he permit them to use all the land on the lower shore, he also gave a great tract of land to "his son" Savage and a great tract of land to Yeardley.

This meeting with "the Laughing King" opened settlement on the Eastern Shore. Yeardley designated land at Ackomack for the new plantation and he placed Captain William Epps in charge. A year and a half later, a colony muster would show seventy-six men, women, and children living "at the Eastern Shore." John and Frances Blore and Captain Wilcocks were still there. And now, Thomas Savage had joined the settlement.

---

[1] In these early years, England still used the Julian or old style (o.s.) calendar in which the legal year began on March 25. In this book, double years are used for dates between January 1 and March 24; the first year is old style and the second year is new style (n.s.) as in 1632/33 (o.s./n.s.).

SPELLING AND SUCH

For old sources such as the *Virginia Company Records of London* or John Smith's *The Generall Historie of Virginia*, I have modernized the spelling of some words, particularly when the old sources used a superscript abbreviation that may not be recognized today. (For example: *ye* with a superscript e was changed to *the*, and *yt* with a superscript t was changed to *that*.) Some antiquated spellings were left intact if they seemed recognizable. Most punctuation (or the lack of) was left intact. For example, I chose to omit the apostrophe in *Dales Gift*, because the early records very rarely (if ever) used that mark.

The names of a few towns have varied spellings, *Kicotan* in particular. In this book, you will see Jamestown written as *James City*, because that was the name used most often in the early records. *Ackomack* is another name that has many spellings. The early court spelled it as *Acchawmacke*. *Accomack* is the spelling used today for the county of that name. I chose to use *Ackomack* as this was Wilcocks's spelling. Because this spelling looks different from most others that are commonly used, perhaps it will help to remind us that this story is not about the land now called Accomack. It is about the land now called Northampton.

REGARDING THE SUBTITLE

In 1942, *The Virginia Magazine of History and Biography* published "Some New Thoughts Concerning the Earliest Settlements on the Eastern Shore of Virginia," an article contributed by two of the Eastern Shore's most esteemed researchers, Anne Floyd Upshur and Ralph T. Whitelaw. It's an article still relevant today, although—as you will see—I take issue with at least one of their conclusions. Forty-one years ago—almost forty years after Upshur and Whitelaw's article was published—I began reading Eastern Shore history. At first, the subject was merely a component of my always-present interest in Virginia history, but over the years, Virginia's Eastern Shore became a primary subject of interest.

Throughout the early years of my reading, the idea never occurred to me that I would one day begin to see a different picture, a reckoning so to speak, of how the Eastern Shore's first permanent English settlement came to be. It was not my intention. I had never doubted the early, venerated writers of Eastern Shore history. I still don't doubt them, but

I have drawn conclusions that are different from some of their findings. This is primarily a result of today's resources which are unlike anything Miss Upshur and Mr. Whitelaw ever imagined. It boggles my mind to think what such minds as theirs could have done with today's internet resources and technology.

All this to say, I am echoing a part of Anne Floyd Upshur and Ralph T. Whitelaw's title, because you will indeed find some new thoughts here. You'll also find some of the old, merely in a different light.

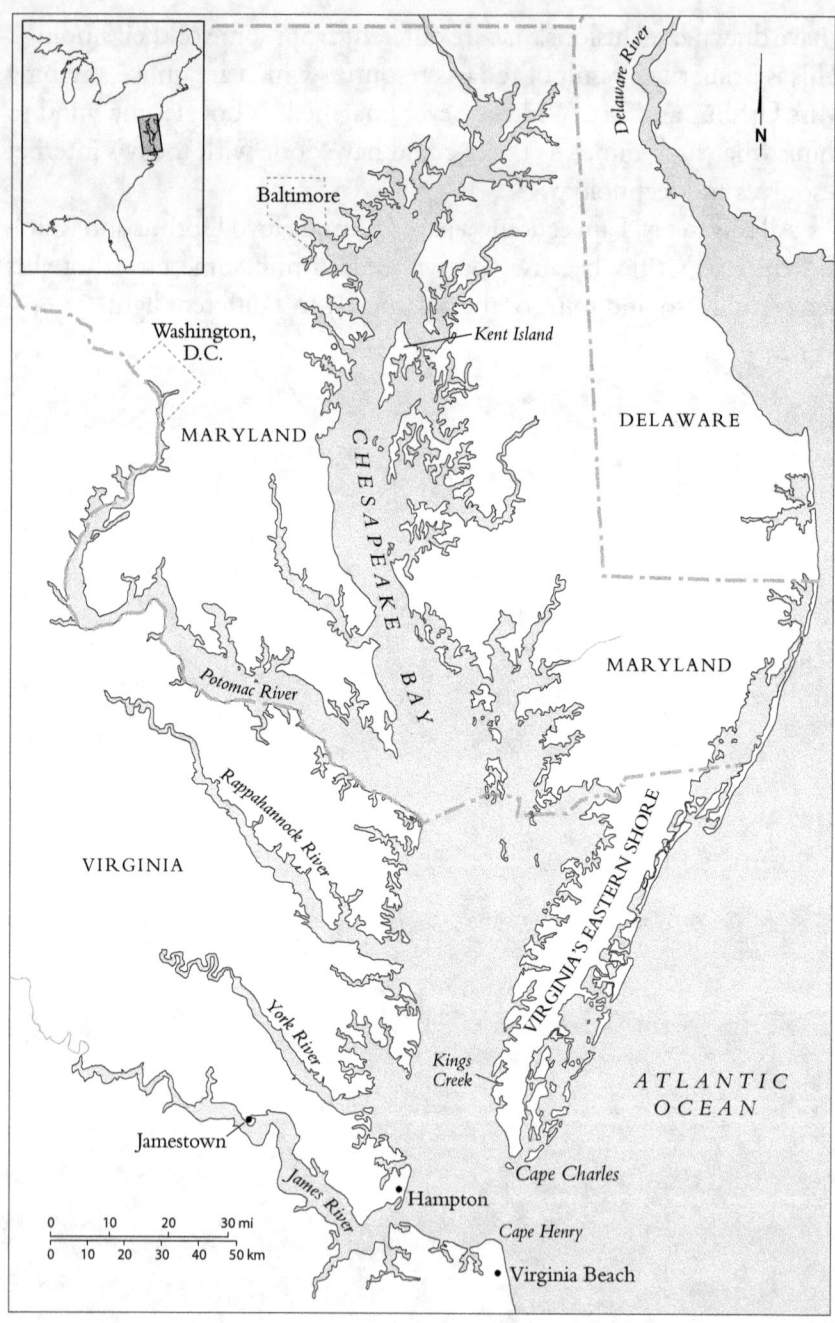

The mighty Chesapeake Bay separates Virginia's Eastern Shore from mainland Virginia. In 1621, Secretary John Pory placed ten men at *Kings Creek*. This creek became the hub of local government in the first two decades of English settlement on the Eastern Shore.

English Boots and Boats

In the midst of what I thought was a careful, painstaking description of the topic of this book, a friend—older and wiser than I—interrupted me. "Wouldn't it be more accurate to just say the Indians were the first settlers?" I did a double-take. What was the motive for such a question? Was I being unclear that my topic was about the first *English* settlers to the Eastern Shore? Was my friend suggesting that I was being insensitive, or—to put it bluntly—racist?

"Well, ah," I stammered in reply, "of course the native people were already here when the English came, but they weren't *English* settlers. I'm writing from what the English records tell us. If I were an archaeologist, I'd be reading the records left by the native people. That's not a story I can tell. I can read English. I can't read the earth. But I don't mean to disregard the story of the native people. I tell what I can about them because they too are in the records. I'm just trying to set the record straight about what the English records tell us about which English people first settled here on this peninsula. There's so much more to that story than what's been told."

My friend sat back in her chair. A wan smile softened her words. "It's just that so many people think it all started with the English. Or the Spanish. Or the Portuguese. I just felt I needed to say that."

It is a point well taken.

I wish this could be a story about the first people to settle on what is today called Virginia's Eastern Shore. That story would begin thousands of years ago and would describe a people that most of us can only imagine. It would describe a land that faintly resembles the land we know today, populated by animals that are familiar and by some we've never seen in our lifetime. The expertise for that story belongs to others; in fact, you will find good books and papers written and being written by those with such expertise. For now, in this story that is taken from the early English records, let's begin by acknowledging—as my friend suggested—that the English were not the first settlers.

~

Virginia's Eastern Shore is at the tapering end of a very large peninsula on the East Coast of the United States. This peninsula is known today as the Delmarva Peninsula because it encompasses most of Delaware, part of Maryland, and part of Virginia. This massive body of land lines the eastern edge of the Chesapeake Bay. The Virginia part of the peninsula is separated from the mainland of Virginia by the Chesapeake Bay, with a span ranging from thirteen to thirty miles across.

To gain entrance into the Chesapeake Bay and its many harbors, a ship would have to pass between the peninsula's most southern cape, called Cape Charles, and Virginia's mainland cape, called Cape Henry. The span between these two capes is thirteen miles of ocean waters. European explorers of the seventeenth century coveted that gateway.

The first Englishman known to have stepped onto a beach of the lower peninsula was Captain Bartholomew Gilbert. On a fatal day in 1603, Gilbert and several crewmen stepped ashore to search for members of Roanoke's lost colony. It was reported that he and some of the crew were killed by men of the native people whom the English called "Indians." Gilbert's remaining crew quickly retreated and sailed straight back to England.[2]

---

[2] Cynthia J. Van Zandt, *Brothers Among Nations: Pursuit of Intercultural Alliances in Early America, 1560-1660* (Oxford University Press, 2008), 50–51. While Gilbert's exploration may have been the first documented English landing, other explorers' writings have suggested earlier landings. For an excellent description of Giovanni da Verrazzano's possible landing on Virginia's Eastern Shore, see Jennings Cropper Wise, *Ye Kingdome of Accawmacke, Or, The Eastern shore of Virginia in the Seventeenth Century* (Richmond: Bell Book, 1911), 6–9.

No one knows where Gilbert's deadly landing took place, but the description suggests it was on Virginia's Eastern Shore. Present-day Northampton County embraced that likelihood and authorized the inclusion of "1603" on its county seal. Gilbert's step ashore represented English leather meeting Virginia sand; thus, Northampton raises a flag for being the "first" in the colony and becoming the birthplace of a nation.[3]

The next Englishman known to have touched the Eastern Shore was Captain John Smith. In June 1608, a year after Jamestown was founded, Smith and fourteen men sailed their "open Barge neare three tuns burthen" from Cape Henry to the Eastern Shore's southern end.[4] At the point named Cape Charles, Smith's group encountered two Indians. These men escorted the Englishmen to Ackomack, home of the werowance, or "king" as the English interpreted the word.

In the village, Smith came face to face with the Indian leader, a man Smith described as "the comliest proper civill Salvage wee incountred." Speaking the language of Powhatan, these people were welcoming, and they supplied Smith with accurate descriptions of the bay, its islands, and its rivers.[5]

The next recorded exploratory party to the Eastern Shore was led by Captain Samuel Argall, an officer of the Virginia colony. In May of 1613, Argall explored this side of the bay for almost two weeks. He later wrote: "We also discovered a multitude of Ilands bearing good Medow ground, and as I thinke, Salt might easily be made there, if there were any ponds digged, for that I found Salt kerned where found water had over-

---

[3] Northampton's county seal includes 1603, commemorating the county as the first place Englishmen stepped ashore in Virginia. The seal also includes 1620 (the year of the first permanent English settlement) and 1634 (the year the county was created by the colonial Grand Assembly).

[4] The group was accompanied by the *Phoenix* at Cape Henry from where Smith and his crew left to begin their exploration in the barge. They returned to the James River in the barge. John Smith, *The Generall Historie of Virginia, New England, & The Summer Isles* (London, 1624, Reprint, Bedford, Ma., Applewood Books, 2006), 115, 123 (hereafter: Smith, *Generall Historie*).

[5] Smith, *Generall Historie*, 115–116. In his account of this 1608 meeting, Smith did not name the Indian werowance. The story of Smith's encounter with the Eastern Shore Indians can also be found in: Kirk Mariner, *True Tales of the Eastern Shore* (Onancock, Va.: Miona Press, 2003), 14–16. *Salvage* was an early spelling of "savage;" a term the early English often used, categorizing the native people as primitive and uncivilized.

flowne in certain places. Here is also great store of fish, both shel-fish and other."[6] (He was speaking, it is thought, of Virginia's barrier islands.)

In that summer of 1613, Captain Ralph Hamor witnessed a frigate load of sturgeon, bass, and other great fish taken at Smith Island. He lamented the lack of salt, saying that if they'd had salt they might have taken enough fish to serve the whole colony for a year.[7]

In 1614, Deputy Governor Sir Thomas Dale commissioned the establishment of an outpost on the Eastern Shore for salt production and fishing. On behalf of the colony, Dale's emissaries acquired land on the lower Eastern Shore from the local Indians. The details are unknown, including the land boundaries, but the tract was named Dales Gift.

---

[6] Purchas, Samuel. *Purchas His Pilgrimes: In Five Bookes* (United Kingdom: n.p., 1625), Vol. 4, 1765. Argall wrote this in a letter to Nicholas Hawes, June 1613.
[7] Ralph Hamor, *A True Discourse of the Present State of Virginia* (Richmond, 1957 [orig. publ. London, 1615]), 21.

John Rolfe's Report

In 1617, John Rolfe was in England with his wife, Rebecca (better known in history by her native name, Pocahontas). The Rolfes and their infant son had embarked from Virginia as part of an entourage, including Sir Thomas Dale and Captain Samuel Argall. Their purpose was to promote the colony on behalf of the discouraged investors of the Virginia Company. This company was the private charter enterprise that was funding the colony. The Rolfes' contribution to promoting Virginia is probably best remembered for two reasons: first and foremost because Pocahontas died while she was still in England and, less well known, because John wrote a descriptive essay about Virginia while he was in England.

In his essay, Rolfe described the Virginia colony as having six inhabited places: Henrico, Bermuda Hundred, West and Sherley Hundred, James Towne, Kequoughtan, and Dales Gift.[8] Henrico operated with 38 men and boys, Bermuda Hundred operated with 119 men, West and Sherley Hundred counted 25 men, James Towne had 50, and Kequoughtan had 20. In addition to the men and working boys, 80 women and children lived throughout the settlements for a total of 351 colonists. "At Dales Gift," Rolfe wrote, "(being upon the sea, neere unto Cape Charles,

---

[8] *Kequoughtan, Kiccowtan, Kicotan,* etc. In these early years, the spelling varied with each writer. This was the same for the name *Henrico* which was also spelled as *Henricus*.

about thirty myles from Kequoughtan,) are seventeen, under the command of one lieutenant Cradock; all these are fedd and maintayned by the colony. Their labor is to make salt and catch fish at the two seasons aforementioned" (spring and fall).[9]

Lieutenant William Cradock commanded these men. Debate regarding the camp's precise location puts it on the bay side, and then on the seaside, but Rolfe noted only that the area was "upon the sea, near unto Cape Charles." Four years later, John Pory, the colony's secretary, corroborated that this location was "over against yt on ye maine," which translates as "over across from it [Smith Island], on the mainland."[10]

Rolfe equated Dales Gift with all other settlements in the colony, including Bermuda Hundred with a population that was seven times greater. At most, the Dales Gift saltworks operated for three years, or six seasons. In February 1617/18, William Cradock was assigned to be Bermuda Hundred's provost marshal; by that time, the saltworks were deserted and the fishing expeditions had moved into the north Atlantic.[11]

For well over 100 years, a small waterway on the lower Eastern Shore retained the name "Craddock Creek," no doubt named after the able lieutenant who oversaw the colony's salt and fishing operation on the lower Eastern Shore. Today a manmade strip of water, the Intracoastal Waterway, cuts through this creek (now called Raccoon). Such reshaping of the land and water hampers the opportunity to stand at creekside and imagine the precise comings and goings of Lieutenant Cradock and his company of fishermen and salt workers, but it is still possible. The exercise is worth a try because the view is extraordinary.[12]

---

[9] John Rolf[e], "A True Relation of the State of Virginia left by Sir Thomas Dale Knight in May last 1616." https://encyclopediavirginia.org/entries/a-true-relation-of-the-state-of-virginia-lefte-by-sir-thomas-dale-knight-in-may-last-1616-1617/

[10] Perry, James R. *The Formation of a Society on Virginia's Eastern Shore, 1615-1655* (Chapel Hill: The University of North Carolina Press, 2012), 15. The word "sea" was used in reference to both the ocean and the bay, so it is of no help in determining the location of Cradock's camp. Pory's description of Smith Island and the mainland of Cape Charles is found in Susan Myra Kingsbury, ed. *The Records of The Virginia Company of London. Vol. I-IV* (Washington, D.C.:Government Printing Office, 1906-1933), 304 (hereafter: Kingsbury, *VCL-1*, *VCL-2*, *VCL-3* or *VCL-4*).

[11] Kingsbury, *VCL-3*, 242.

[12] The Eastern Shore of Virginia National Wildlife Refuge (http://www.fws.gov/refuge/eastern_shore_of_virginia/).

Captain George Yeardley

When Deputy Governor Sir Thomas Dale departed Virginia in 1616 along with the Rolfes and Argall, he left Captain Yeardley as his deputy in charge of the colony. By this time, Yeardley had been a colonist for six years.

George Yeardley could have followed his father into the profession of merchant tailoring in London, but he had chosen instead to become a soldier. While serving in the Low Countries during England's assistance to the Dutch in their war with Spain, Yeardley apparently earned the respect of his commander, Sir Thomas Gates. An original Virginia Company investor, Gates was appointed in 1609 to be Virginia's new governor. When Gates traveled to the colony on the Third Supply, Yeardley accompanied him as part of the governor's guard. Both men were aboard the supply's flagship, the *Sea Venture*, when it foundered in a fierce storm and wrecked on Bermuda. The exciting tale of that event is the subject of books and articles, so suffice it to say they finally made it to Virginia about nine months later. By that time, the ninety or so survivors of the colony were in wretched shape. Most were starving. Those months preceding Gates's arrival have been termed "the Starving Time" in Jamestown's history.

In the next few years, Yeardley was promoted to captain of the guard and served the colony well. When Ralph Hamor wrote his 1614 discourse on Virginia, he noted that George Yeardley was next in command to Sir Thomas Dale at Bermuda Hundred, the largest of the new plantations.

In May 1617, Captain Samuel Argall returned to Virginia to take the position of Deputy Governor while all awaited the arrival of Virginia's lifetime governor, Thomas West, 3rd Baron De La Warr. In October 1618, word reached England that Lord De La Warr had died en route to the colony.

Lord De La Warr had been appointed governor in 1610. He was the man who rescued the colony after the Starving Time, but he fell ill and left Virginia in 1611. Over the next seven years, his place was held by a series of deputy governors. Lord De La Warr's death prompted the Virginia Company to make significant changes in the colony's management.

Within a month of learning about Lord De La Warr's death, the Virginia Company selected Captain George Yeardley to be the new governor of Virginia. The appointment of governors would be for three-year terms, not for life as had been the case with Lord De La Warr.

Yeardley's appointment was not unanimously supported. Most of the Company leadership preferred a nobleman or an experienced knight for the governorship, but the man they would have chosen—Sir Thomas Dale—was commanding a fleet on behalf of the East India Company. When King James knighted Yeardley a few days after the appointment, many Company investors were highly offended. This dissonance would follow Yeardley into Virginia and plague him as he attempted to meet the challenges put on him by the Company.[13]

The Virginia Company's directive to Governor Yeardley has come to be known as "the Great Charter" because it forged a plan to recreate the colony in the image of England.[14] Now, instead of military rule, the colony would be guided by English common law. Thousands of acres of Company land would be surveyed and worked by Company tenants. These tenants were men whose passage had been paid by the Company after the time when Sir Thomas Dale left the colony. These men would work the land for seven years and receive half the profit. The other half

---

[13] Kingsbury, *VCR-3*, 217. Great Britain, William Noel Sainsbury et al., *Calendar of State Papers, Colonial Series, 1574–1660* (London: 1860), 20 (hereafter: Sainsbury, *Calendar*).

[14] Kingsbury, *VCR-3*, 98–109.

of the profit would go to support the colony management, including securing and wintering the public cattle stock and paying officers to oversee the Company land and its tenants. "Ancient Adventurers and Planters" who came to Virginia at their own costs (before Dale left) and stayed three years would receive 100 acres plus 100 more for each Company share they owned. Planters who came to the colony at the Company's expense before Dale would receive 100 acres after they completed their years of service to the colony on the common land. Planters who came after Dale at their own expense would receive fifty acres.

For better administrative management, the Great Charter divided the colony into four boroughs: Jamestown, Charles City, Henrico, and Kiccowtan. Each of these boroughs would have 3,000 acres of Company land to be worked by Company tenants. Any Company tenants who already lived on this land could stay on the land. Any private person who, in good faith, lived on the Company land would not be moved until he was reimbursed for his costs by the profits from the land. After that, he would have to move.

You may think I've just told you more than you wanted to know, but to understand how the first permanent settlement on Virginia's Eastern Shore came to be, it is necessary to know what Yeardley faced when he took the reins of Virginia as governor. The Great Charter inspired a grand vision for Virginia, but it was an administrative nightmare.

Yeardley was thirty or thirty-one years old when the Virginia Company selected him for the governorship. He was a husband and the father of a baby girl. Yeardley had married Temperance Flowerdew who is well-known today as one of the survivors of the Starving Time. She had come to Virginia on Captain John Martin's ship, the *Falcon*, of the Third Supply.

English records show that a woman named Temperance Flowerdew married a man named Richard Barrow just a few weeks before the Third Supply set sail for Virginia. It is believed that this couple traveled together on the *Falcon*, but nothing more has ever been heard about Richard Barrow, and nothing more is heard about Temperance until she was George Yeardley's wife. We don't even know when and where the Yeardleys married. The best that can be said about the next event in Temperance's life after arriving in 1609 on the *Falcon* is that she gave birth to a daughter, Elizabeth Yeardley, in the year 1619, in Virginia.[15] That's ten years of her life for which we can say nothing. Some writers have suggested that she returned to England and met Yeardley there, but really, no one knows.

Someone recently told me that a current television series about early Jamestown portrays Sir George Yeardley as mean. I winced upon hearing this because I had made the same error years ago as an inexperienced reader of the old records. Note the following quote about George Yeardley: "Here be two or three ships redy for Virginia, and one Captain Yardley a meane fellow by way of provision goes as governor…"[16] After countless hours of reading seventeenth-century English, I learned that this quote does indeed call Yeardley a mean man, but I also know that the word "meane" here speaks to Yeardley's assets. This sentence called attention to Yeardley's lack of resources (including his "low birth"). The writer continued: "… and to grace him the more the King knighted him this weeke at Newmarket."

In seventeenth-century England, hierarchy based on factors of birth meant everything. The top rung of this ladder was the king. Next were the peerage: the dukes, the marquesses, the earls, the viscounts, and the barons. Following the peerage came baronets, knights, esquires, gentlemen, and lastly, misters. After that were the many people with no title at all. Before George Yeardley was knighted, he carried the military title of Captain.[17] After his knighthood, he was called Sir George. Temperance was called Lady Yeardley.

The issue of being "meane," or poor and of low birth, was a foreseen problem, so why did the Virginia Company choose Yeardley? The answer to that question may seem trite, but he was in the right place at the right time as the best man for the job. Consider these factors: The noble governor, Lord De La Warr, had just died en route to Virginia; the last knighted governor, Sir Thomas Dale, was out of the country on assignment; and the present governor, Captain Samuel Argall, had

---

[15] The James City 1624/25 muster shows that Elizabeth was 6 years old when that muster was taken, and that she had been born in Virginia. It is, of course, possible that she was born in 1618.
[16] Chamberlain, John, 1554?-1628, and Norman Egbert McClure. *The Letters of John Chamberlain*. Philadelphia: The American philosophical society, 1939, 188.
[17] Yeardley was designated by his military rank in his 1618 commission ("the Great Charter").

essentially been recalled to London to answer charges of misusing Company resources for his own profit. Captain Yeardley was in London and immediately available.

The then top man in the Virginia Company, Treasurer Sir Thomas Smyth, had been particularly offended when Yeardley was knighted. Yeardley's greatest source of support within the Company was Deputy Treasurer Sir Edwin Sandys who assured the Virginia Company investors of Yeardley's "faithfulness, experience, and industry."[18] Within four months after Yeardley's departure for Virginia, Sandys would be elected Treasurer; from this position, he could better cushion criticism of the newly knighted governor.

Upon the occasion of Yeardley's knighting at Newmarket, King James and Yeardley had a conversation about Virginia. Thankfully, part of the exchange was recorded by a courtier. I add the story here, not because it advances our knowledge of settlement on the Eastern Shore, but because it brings a bit of color and feeling to these two men on a day now long passed. According to the courtier, the king said that Yeardley "proved very understanding." In their conversation, Yeardley told the king that the native people of Virginia "do believe in the resurrection of the body; and that when the body dies, the soul goes into certain fair pleasant fields, there to solace itself until the end of the world, and then the soul is to return to the body again, and they shall live both together happily and perpetually." Upon hearing this, the king commented "that the gospel must have been heretofore known in that country, though it be lost, and this fragment only remains."[19]

It was one of those conversations that both men surely remembered and pondered from time to time throughout the rest of their lives.

---

[18] Kingsbury, *VCR-3*, 216–218.
[19] Alexander Brown, *The First Republic in America* (Cambridge: Riverside Press, 1898), 293–294. The courtier was Philip Mainwaring.

Samuel Argall in negotiation with the Chickahominy by Johann Theodore de Bry.

In the Wake of Captain Argall

Deputy Governor Samuel Argall still held sway in the colony when the Virginia Company appointed George Yeardley as governor. In April 1619, when Yeardley was two weeks off the coast of Virginia, Argall left James City to return to England. It is said that he left to avoid being arrested and sent back in irons.[20]

When you read about what was happening in the Virginia Company at this time, you may come across statements that characterize Yeardley and Argall as enemies. Some will say that Yeardley accused Argall of malfeasance and hotly pursued evidence with which to convict him. You might read that Yeardley's greatest advocate in the Company, Sir Edwin Sandys, drummed up the charges against Argall in order to make Treasurer Sir Thomas Smyth look bad and wrest the Company's leadership role for himself. However, Sandys addressed this fallacy when he cited a 1618 letter to Lord De La Warr from Thomas Smyth,

---

[20] Connor, Seymour V. "Sir Samuel Argall: A Biographical Sketch." *The Virginia Magazine of History and Biography* 59, no. 2 (1951): 173. Accessed March 23, 2021. http://www.jstor.org/stable/4245766.

Robert Johnson, John Wolstenholm, and John Danvers. In this letter, written before anyone thought to make George Yeardley governor, the Company leadership asked Lord De La Warr to send Argall back to address the "many misdemeanors of his for which he must make satisfaction to the Company."[21] And then Lord De La Warr died en route to Virginia before such an action could be taken.

It is highly unlikely that Yeardley and Argall were enemies. Two years into his governorship, Yeardley and his councilors were sitting "till midnight," examining witnesses concerning Argall's alleged malfeasance, and yet near this same time, Yeardley named his newborn child "Argall."[22] This could mean (though not necessarily) that the Yeardleys intended for Samuel Argall to be the godfather of Argall Yeardley. If Sir George and Lady Temperance held Captain Argall in such high regard that they gave his name to their first son, imagine Yeardley's anguish when carrying out the Company's orders to find evidence against this family friend. Despite any feelings of friendship, Yeardley was faithful to his assignment.

Captain Argall was accused of having caused "great losses" to the Company by "misimploying their Tenants, Corne, Cattle and other yearly proffits in the time of his Government to his owne private ends and gayne."[23] Upon arriving in Virginia, Yeardley found that most of the men who could reasonably testify that Argall "hath wrought Craftily and dishonestly in all his proceedings" had been won over by Argall.[24] At the direction of the Company, Governor Yeardley spent countless hours attempting to bring order to the colony's accounts while trying to uncover actionable evidence against Argall. The Company also spent countless hours combing through reports in England about Argall, but a trial never materialized.

On an unknown day in Yeardley's first year as governor, eight men in England (Thomas Gates, Francis West, Samuel Argall, Daniel Tucker, Dr. Lawrence Bohun, Robert Beheathland, Rogier Smyth, and James Swift) each put his signature to a letter asking for a different Virginia

---

[21] Kingsbury, *VCR-2*, 55.
[22] Kingsbury, *VCR-3*, 417. Argall Yeardley's birth is determined from the 1624/25 muster. He was four years old in January 1624/25; therefore, his birth would have been in 1620 or 1621. A spelling often used for the son's name is "Argoll."
[23] Kingsbury, *VCR-2*, 27.
[24] Kingsbury, *VCR-3*, 119.

leader. They wished for someone such as the deceased Lord De La Warr, a man who could "hold up the dignity of so Great and good a cause."[25]

Gates had been his commander in the early years of the colony; Argall and West had been colleagues. Francis West was a brother of the deceased Lord De La Warr. Were these men specifically against Yeardley as governor, or was it a matter of believing that the head of the colony should have noble qualities that a mere title could not possibly imbue? Whatever it was, this viewpoint from these men surely added to the weight pressing down on Governor Sir George Yeardley.

---

[25] Kingsbury, VCR-3, 231. John Smith cast Yeardley in an unfavorable light and portrayed Argall as nearly heroic. According to Smith, Yeardley was ineffective as a leader and prone to look after his own interests (see Smith, *Generall Historie*, 240, 302). However, the records of the Virginia Company reveal failings in the character of each man, but neither emerges as a villain nor a hero. Smith was not a primary player in the colony after he left in 1609 and probably took his cues in this instance from factions that disfavored Yeardley.

Kings Creek, 1952. Pory placed ten tenants on the Secretary's Land (500 acres on the north shore, center of photograph). [North is to the left in the above photo.] Used by permission: NETRonline, www.historicaerials.com.

Secretary John Pory

In the Company's haste to appoint a governor after the death of Lord De La Warr, it also hastened to appoint a secretary for the colony. At the suggestion of Yeardley, the Company chose John Pory for the position. Pory's three-year term would coincide with Yeardley's. The day after Pory was appointed, he noted in a letter that Yeardley's wife was his "cousin German" and that Yeardley very much enjoyed his company. Pory characterized the Company's offer of an allowance to be "as dry as Pumystones," but Yeardley had assured him that he would receive as much as £200 a year and offered him a loan of £50 to prepare for the voyage.[26]

We are fortunate to have John Pory's letters for their glimpses of colonial life and its people; however, at first, Pory did not relish this assignment. He would much rather have stayed in England to be in the service of someone of the peerage.[27] Sir Edwin Sandys cautioned Yeardley about employing Pory, but Yeardley justified his reasons. Two years into the governorship, Yeardley would reiterate to Sandys his trust in Pory, but he would also note that "nessitty hath no law and better a

---

[26] Brown, *The First Republic*, 294. This letter was to Dudley Carleton, 1st Viscount Dorchester.
[27] Kingsbury, *VCR-3*, 222.

bad foole than none or worse."[28] Clearly this governor and his secretary did not have a stable relationship.

Pory's letters reflect that he resented having to take this job. With no better offer, he embellished his new post, describing it as "Secretary of Estate, the first that ever was chosen and appointed by Commission from the Counsell and Company in England, under their handes & common seale." Still, he was not entirely vain nor crippled by his discontent. His observations of Virginia show that the land at times beguiled him: "Among these Christall rivers, & odoriferous woods I doe escape muche expense, envye, contempte, vanity, and vexation of minde." He seems to have resented his benefactor—the husband of his German cousin—but it wasn't an airtight resentment. On the one hand, Pory could tell of Yeardley's needless jealousies against him, and on the other, he could note that there was "a great deal of worth" in Yeardley's person.[29] Pory seemed often to drop slights regarding Yeardley, but ironically, these bits of information allow us to see into Yeardley's character and work ethic. For example, Pory wrote that Yeardley "constantly avowes and Justifies every iota and title."[30] From this, we can imagine a man who overworked details, no doubt adding more stress to an already stressful job.

Secretary John Pory figures significantly into the story of how a permanent English settlement was placed on Virginia's Eastern Shore, but he is probably best known for his role in the first General Assembly that took place in Jamestown between July 30 and August 4 of 1619. In the preliminary proceedings of this historic event, Pory was appointed as Speaker and his seat was to the front of the governor. From his notes and other papers, Pory wrote a report of that first General Assembly.[31] His report provides vivid details of those ground-breaking five days when twenty-two men came together from eleven settlements to form what history would characterize as America's oldest continuous representative legislature in the Western Hemisphere.[32]

---

[28] Kingsbury, *VCR-3*, 126.
[29] Kingsbury, *VCR-3*, 251, 222.
[30] Kingsbury, *VCR-3*, 251. Pory no doubt was referencing Matthew 5:18 and meant to spell "tittle." A tittle is an old word for the superscript dot over the letter *i*. The phrase "iota and tittle" indicates attention to the smallest detail.
[31] Kingsbury, *VCR-3*, 153–179.
[32] Jamestown Rediscovery, "The First General Assembly," historic-jamestowne.org.

All of the eleven settlements involved in this first General Assembly were on Virginia's mainland: James City, Charles City, City of Henricus, Kiccowtan, Martin Brandon, Smyth's Hundred, Martin's Hundred, Argall's Guiffe, Flowerdieu Hundred, Captain Lawne's plantation, and Captain Warde's plantation. An Eastern Shore settlement did not exist at the time of the first General Assembly.[33]

By September 1619, after less than a half year on the job, Governor George Yeardley informed the Company leadership that he had no interest in continuing as governor after his three years were completed, but that he would be willing to manage the private plantation known as "Smyth's hundred." Sir Edwin Sandys felt that Yeardley's decision was based in fear of being disgraced by Sir Thomas Smyth's "malignancie" toward him. The issue of this ill will seemed to be not at all about Yeardley's abilities, but rather about his "unduely procured Knighthood." Sandys hoped that Yeardley, upon learning of Smyth's departure from the Company, would change his mind about another term.[34]

Sandys was now Treasurer, the chief officer of the Company, but for only one year. Due to his contentious relationship with the king, Sandys withdrew himself from the ballot for reelection. However, he aligned himself with the Earl of Southampton who won the election, and essentially, Sandys continued to direct the affairs of the Virginia Company.

In May 1620, the Company made two decisions that would inadvertently affect settlement on the Eastern Shore. The first was Secretary John Pory's compensation. Governor Yeardley and the Virginia council had sent a schedule of secretary's fees to be approved by the

---

[33] An error in the introduction of Nell Nugent's first volume of Virginia land-patent abstracts may have led some researchers astray on this matter. Nugent reported that the first General Assembly had two Eastern Shore representatives, Captain Ward and Lieutenant Gibbs; however, this statement is inaccurate. Nell Marion Nugent, Virginia Genealogical Society, and Virginia State Library, *Cavaliers And Pioneers: Abstracts of Virginia Land Patents And Grants, 1623-1800, Vol. 1* (Richmond: Press of the Dietz Print Co., 1934), xxi, (hereafter: Nugent, *Vol. 1*). Captain John Ward's plantation was on the James River. Nugent may have made the assumption that Ward was from the Eastern Shore based on where his remaining servants were in 1622, after William Epps rescued them and took them to the Eastern Shore. (Scant evidence suggests that Ward may have been among the fishermen assigned to the Eastern Shore, but at the time of the Assembly, that fishing operation was defunct.)

[34] Kingsbury, *VCR-3*, 216–217.

Company leadership, but the Company found the fees so "intollerable" that it decided the secretary "should have no fees att all." Instead of fees, the Company would allow the secretary's position "certaine Land and tenants" for his compensation. The Company opted to provide 500 acres and twenty tenants for the secretary's position. The charter for this provision would be confirmed in June 1620.[35] The idea was that the twenty tenants would work the land for half the profits and the other half would go to the secretary.

The second decision that would have an effect on Eastern Shore settlement was the appointment of two deputies to govern the Company's lands. The Company had heard and acted on Yeardley's concerns that the scope of governing Virginia was too broad for one man, especially during an investigation of a former governor's activities. The College Land at Henrico would be overseen by Deputy George Thorpe who was already in Virginia. Other Company lands and tenants (not including the Governor's) would be overseen by Deputy Thomas Nuce whose arrival in the fall of 1620 was accompanied by John Wilcocks. No records have revealed whether Nuce and Wilcocks knew one another before their voyage to Virginia; however, two years later, Wilcocks would write his will and name Nuce as an estate overseer. Trust doesn't get much greater than that.

---

[35] Kingsbury, *VCR-1*, 349, 382.

The Broadside

The Company released a lengthy broadside on May 17, 1620. Broadsides were generally a one-page poster featuring a combination of print and pictures. They were printed on cheap paper to be posted or plastered in public places as a means of announcement or advertisement. The purpose of this particular broadside seems to have been twofold: to attract new colonists and to instruct the Virginia leadership in what was expected of them. London tradesmen may have perused the posters in guildhalls while common workers would have caught sight of the bold print pasted upon walls on their everyday paths. Bold woodblock images of arable land, neat cottages, and abundant tables would tap into most anyone's longing for a better life. The Company needed people willing to work.

It's interesting that this particular broadside was released a month before the Company elections took place. Was it a political tool of the present chief officer, Treasurer Sir Edwin Sandys, or was it an annual report? Perhaps it was a combination of such undertakings meant to inspire investment. The Company was in desperate need of money and labor. Such a publication might inspire confidence in the Virginia project, thus enticing new investors and new colonists.

The broadside began with an acknowledgement that the colony had just experienced a year of high mortality. These deaths, the Company said, were a necessary punishment from "the just finger of Almighty God." The Company advised the colony, as well as itself, to show contrition through such acts as "better attending the divine worship, and more carefully observing his holy and just Lawes, to worke a reconciliation, and to entreate the renewing of his most gracious favour towards us."

On the other hand, the Company noted, the high mortality was caused by a disease that did not kill seasoned inhabitants and wouldn't have killed the new ones if they had been given better provisions against such sickness. The broadside then detailed a requirement for each of the four boroughs and the plantations to build a "guesthouse" for the lodging of fifty people. Such houses were sometimes called "hospitals" in the sense that they were to be hospitable havens for newcomers and visitors. The housing for newcomers had been a problem, and as the Company planned to send more laborers to support the colony, it wanted the colony to do its part to provide housing. Reports of homelessness and people dying in the woods for lack of shelter did not attract new people. "Guesthouse" had the sound of an invitation.

Each guesthouse was to be 16x108 feet with five chimneys and windows enough for air. Along each long wall were to be twenty-five bedsteads, each 4x6 feet and 2 feet high off the ground. Wooden partitions would separate each bed. The costs, labor, and materials would be at the common expense of each borough or plantation, but for its part, the Company was giving each borough or plantation two heifers to begin a common stock on the common land.

Each borough and plantation was to have at least one "godly and learned minister." Ministers for the boroughs and for the Company lands would be provided by the Company, while plantations would provide their own ministers. The governor would provide the minister for the Governor's Land, and the college investors would provide for the College Land. All ministers would follow the laws of the Church of England. Each minister would be provided six tenants to work his 100-acre glebe lands; for the Company, Governor's, and College Lands, the Company would provide the minister's tenants. For the boroughs and the plantations, the Company would provide three of the six tenants. Ministers would be responsible for maintaining the number of six tenants and these would be passed on to their ministerial successors.

The Company committed to building up the colony by supplying 600 people for public use and asked that the colony help the new arrivals. The new tenants would need housing and "other necessary reliefe and succour." The Company noted that it could require this "one-time" assistance, but had thought better of that strategy and instead would "try the love of the Colony." (In other words, the Company was asking the colonists to shoulder—in all good faith—the hardship imposed on them by the Company's overly ambitious importation of colonists.)

Lastly, but probably not least of its concerns, the Company addressed commodities. Tobacco as the sole commodity was a disgrace upon the colony and upon the country. Colonists had abandoned other crops and trades in order to grow tobacco, apparently thinking it was the way to wealth. However, tobacco could not sustain life; what good was cash if no one was producing food or building houses? The broadside then reiterated the Company's promotion of "reall Commodities." It expounded upon its objectives for the production of iron, cordage, pitch and tar, timber, silk, vines, and salt. (Corn and cattle would not be used as commodities as they were needed for the colony's sustenance.) Of the sixty-seven lines of type devoted to the seven commodities, more than a third spoke to the production of salt. The Company's promotion of salt at this time in history has a bearing on the Eastern Shore story. (In the following excerpt from the broadside, spelling has been selectively modernized.)

> "*The last commodity*, but not of least importance for health, is SALT: the works whereof having been lately suffered to decay; we now intending to restore in so great plenty, as not only to serve the Colony for the present, but as is hoped, in short time, the great fishings on those Coasts (a matter of inestimable advancement to the Colony) do upon mature deliberation ordain as followeth: first, that you the Governour and Councell, doe chose out of the Tenants for the Company, 20. fit persons to be employed in saltworks, which are to be renewed in *Smiths Iland*, where they were before; as also in taking of Fish there, for use of the Colony, as in former time was also done. These 20. shall be furnished out at the first, at the charges of the Company, with all implements and instruments necessary for those works. They shall have also assigned to each of them,

for their occupation or use, 50. acres of Land, within the same Iland, to be the Land of the Company. The one moiety of *Salt, Fish*, and profits of the Land, shall be for the Tenants, and the other for us the Company, to be delivered into our Store: and this contract shall be to continue for five years. We doe also hereby grant and ordain, that if any of the old Burroughs, or other particular *Plantations*, shall be pleased to concur in the same works of making *Salt*, and taking *Fish*, they shall be admitted thereunto to the number of twenty persons or under, for every Burrough or *Plantation*, with the like Grants as before, & with the same Divisions of profit, between them and their Landlords, as is before set down between the Company and their Tenants."[36]

Thus, the Company wanted the Smith Island salt and fishing operation to resume. The governor and council would choose twenty Company men, equip them, give them each fifty acres on the island and, for five years, allow them half profits of the salt, fish, and the land. It sounded ideal but when the former salters heard of it, their reaction was unexpected.

---

[36] Kingsbury, *VCR-3*, 275–280.

Pory's Opinion

Almost a month after the May 1620 broadside was published in England, Secretary John Pory in Virginia wrote a letter to Sir Edwin Sandys and addressed most of the broadside's issues. From his response, it appears that drafts of the broadside had arrived by several ships that came to Virginia that spring. Pory sent his response out on the *Duty* which left James City in June. If Pory and other officers had expected the Company to consider their viewpoints before publication, they were sorely disappointed. It would be interesting to know how Pory's letter was adjudged by the Company, because now, 400 years later, it makes the London leadership appear foolhardy, if not foolish.

Pory said that building guesthouses at this time of year was "most unfitting." The timber needed to be felled, but the trees were full of sap. Besides, he stated, people were attending to their corn at this time. Winter was a better time for such a project. Pory was critical of suggestions that old planters could assist with the projects. On this subject, Pory reveals something of Yeardley's protective nature and generosity: "The Governor if he were able would defray all these public affairs out of his own purse, and would not put the people to so much as an hours work." Yeardley had offered his salary toward the building of a fort at Point Comfort; Pory suggested that the Company could apply that offer to the building of guesthouses and other public works.

Of interest to the English founding of Virginia's Eastern Shore, Pory wrote about the plans for "Smiths Iland." With some backdoor bragging about his extensive travels, Pory assured the Company that he knew how more salt could be made by the heat of the sun (the method used in France, Spain, and Italy) than "by that toylesome and erroneous way of boyling sea water into salt in kettles" (the method formerly used at Smith Island).

Pory then told Sir Edwin that men who knew "Smiths Iland" were laughing at the Company's plan to give fifty acres on the island to each tenant:

> Whereas the company doe give their tennants fifty acres upon Smyths Iland some there are that smyle at it here, sayinge there is no ground in all the whole Iland worth the manuringe. But over against it on the maine, which Sir Thomas Dale bought from the Indyans for the company, there is as good ground as any is in Virginia, and such a place to live in by the reporte of those that have bene there as (savinge the incomodity of Musquitos, which the ground beinge once cleared will vanish) the like is skarce to be found againe in the whole country. And for my partycular, I was never so enamoured of any place which I have not seene, nor shalbe satisfyed till I have seene it.

Having heard the stories of men who had been to the Eastern Shore, Pory was smitten. He dreamed of seeing the land for himself, but as of June 12, 1620, he hadn't been there. Later that month in England, the Company approved the charter for Pory's position to receive 500 acres of land and twenty tenants in lieu of fees for his work. While the Company had plans to send half of those tenants in the current year, a full year would pass before any tenants arrived.

Pory had given a great deal of thought to all subjects pertaining to the success of the colony. He was often bold in his comments and—given that the Company was so slow to provide him any means of compensation—this is understandable. His comments pertaining to iron were particularly candid and, for that reason, more insightful than those of most other men of the day. With great candor, Pory told Sir Edwin that it was the colony's general opinion that—since iron production in the colony was so important—the Company should have spent more time planning how to go about establishing an iron works in Virginia. The Company, he said, should have sent a skilled man who could have taken a full year to study the country and its resources as no one in Virginia had experience with iron.[37]

For years the Company had hammered away at the Virginians, pleading with them to produce iron. This desperate search for iron would have a bearing on the Eastern Shore's first permanent settlement in an unexpected way.

---

[37] Kingsbury, *VCR-3*, 300–306.

Deputy Thomas Nuce

On May 17, 1620 (the same date as the broadside), the Virginia Company appointed Captain Thomas Nuce to take charge of the Company's lands and tenants. Four months later, Deputy Nuce took passage on the *Bona Nova* to arrive in Virginia in October.[38]

According to the Great Charter, the Company's public lands included 3,000 acres each at Henrico, Charles City, Kicotan, and Jamestown. The governor looked after the Governor's Land, and by this time, Deputy George Thorpe was already in Virginia supervising the College Land at Henrico. Instead of fees or a salary, Nuce's position was allowed 1,200 acres (600 at Kicotan, 400 at Charles City, 100 at Henrico, and 100 at James City) and forty tenants. Twenty tenants were sent over with him and the Company planned to send twenty more over the next two springs. (A year later, the Company would add ten to the number—when willing men could be procured—for a total of fifty tenants contracted to work the deputy's lands for seven years.)[39]

We know where Nuce made his home, because eight months after Nuce's arrival to Virginia, the Company instructed the new minister, Mr. Bolton, to live with the Nuce family in Elizabeth City (the settlement

---

[38] Kingsbury, *VCR-3*, 375, 406.
[39] Kingsbury, *VCR-1*, 340.

formerly called Kicotan).[40] The Company had instructed Nuce to begin his duties at Elizabeth City, so it made sense that he would reside there. The Company land in Elizabeth City was located "att the Cominge in of the River."[41] The main river was known as Southampton, later shortened to Hampton. "Coming in at the river" translates to today's location of Hampton's VA hospital and Hampton University.

Deputy Nuce had not arrived in time to relieve the governor's burden of finding homes and food for the hundreds of new arrivals to the colony that year. While the Company had been discussing the appointment of deputies to help oversee its lands and people, Governor Sir George Yeardley's usual self-deprecating composure finally broke. On June 7, 1620, Yeardley had penned a letter to Treasurer Sir Edwin Sandys.

> There lying at this present upon my shoulders so great a burthen that I am not able to looke into all particulars so sodaynly [suddenly] as this Ship will depart, this great number of people also ariving Enexpected it hath not a littell pusseled me to provide for the lodging of them, it being a thing of spetiall consequence and nessesity for theire healths, but herein I must acknowledge your care and zeale for the hasty and speedy erecting this good worke, in sending so many people for sondry profitable employments in Each where of I doe here passe my promise unto you, and hould my selfe bound to doe my best endever, and had not your zealous desires over hasted you and the passage at sea bin Soe unfortunate to the duty, whereby I had no warning at all given to provide for these people, I should have bine able to have done much better then now I can, yett I beseech God to give a blessing to my endevors, they are now all loged [lodged] within good houses as this Country doth afforde not one but lyeth upon a bed stead high from the ground and have their victualls well dressed...[42]

---

[40] Kingsbury, *VCR-3*, 485. The Virginia Company was using the new name by May 17, 1620; see Kingsbury, *VCR-1*, 349.
[41] Kingsbury, *VCR-1*, 340.
[42] Kingsbury, *VCR-3*, 297.

Sir George went on to say that he had added peas, oatmeal, and biscuits to the provisions of the new arrivals and he had sent the bill to the Company. He explained that the provision of grain that came with the new colonists was too harsh on a newcomer. The variety he would provide, including Indian corn, was more healthful. Fish and flesh for the many new arrivals couldn't be obtained readily, so each new arrival would be allowed more of the provisions to compensate.

These four hundred years later, Yeardley's exasperation and disappointment leach from the page. With adequate notice, he said, the colony could have prepared for the newcomers. He reminded Sandys that summer was unhealthy for travel and arrival. At least one hundred people, he said, had come ashore weak, sick, or crazy. "And now this great heate of weather striketh many more."

A good deal of the men sent for the iron works had died at sea, and for those who were left, not much could be accomplished in the summer. The "boatwright" died soon after landing, so they had no one to make a shallop that would carry people and provisions up the river. Yeardley used his own shallop instead.

The Company had calculated that the provisions they sent would last six months, but Yeardley's calculations said ten weeks. In addition, the clothes allowance was short. "The people are ready to mutinere," Yeardley wrote.

Ironically, on that same day in England, Sir Edwin Sandys wrote a letter to the Marquis of Buckingham, patting himself on the back for doing more "in my one yeare, with lesse then Eight Thousand pounds, for the advancement of that Colonie in People & store of Commodities, then was doon [done] in Sir Thomas Smiths Twelve yeares, with expence of neer Eightie Thousand pounds."[43]

A half-year or less after Nuce's arrival and almost a year after Yeardley's searing letter, Deputy Thomas Nuce penned his own weighty concerns to Sir Edwin Sandys. By this time, Sir Edwin was no longer the top man in the Company, but he still had great influence. Nuce's letter describes conditions at Elizabeth City in 1621.

---

[43] Kingsbury, *VCR-3*, 295. George Villiers was the Marquis of Buckingham at that time.

> I assure yow[you] the people lyve [live] very barely for the most part: havinge no other foode but bread & water and such manner of meate as they make of the Mayze: which I would to God I Could say they had in any reasonable plenty. I assure yow the world goes hard with many even at this tyme. The labor is infynite that they are here putto for Corne yeerly. In so much that it takes up att the least three parts of our hands. Which if you Consider, yow will not wonder that so great works as yow expect to be done have so slowe progresse…How so many people sent hither of late yeers have bene lost, I cannot Conceave unles it be through water and want, partly of good foode, but cheifly of good Lodginge: which have bene the onely [only] Causes of death of so many as came with me, if the Conceipt [concept] of their 7. years servitude did not help them on: which Course, I am of opinion, yow should doe well to alter. The half yeere, for which onely wee were victualled, since our landinge, is now allmost expyred; sure I am, our provisions are expended, and yet wee here [hear] of no supplie. In so much that yf [if] the Edwin had not stood us in some stead by fetchinge us corne forth of the Bay (wher now we have good and free trade) wee had bene distrest [distressed]. For your provisions fall exceedinge short, which is not my Complaint alone.[44]

The Company was expecting "great works" in commodities other than tobacco. Iron and salt topped the list. In this letter, Nuce very gently—but plainly—described why progress in commodities was so slow. Not only did corn take a great part of their labor, but people were dying. Nuce had been studying the problem of what was killing people. He noted water, food and shelter, but he also cited a psychological disparagement brought on by the anticipation of seven years of servitude. (Nuce would later propose to change from a share-cropping model to one of pensions.[45]) When Nuce died two years later after a long illness, a factor of his death was said to be "the breaking of his hart" that so many of his people had died.[46]

---

[44] Kingsbury, *VCR-3*, 455–456.
[45] Kingsbury, *VCR-3*, 647; *VCR-4*, 185. "Pensions" in this case would have been as an allowance or a guaranteed salary.
[46] Kingsbury, *VCR-4*, 232.

In his letter, Nuce noted that "good and free trade" was coming "forth of the Bay." This probably was a reference to the Eastern Shore as well as to points northward into the Potomac. Nuce was looking for solutions to sustain the Company's many tenants, particularly his own and all others newly arrived and arriving at Elizabeth City.

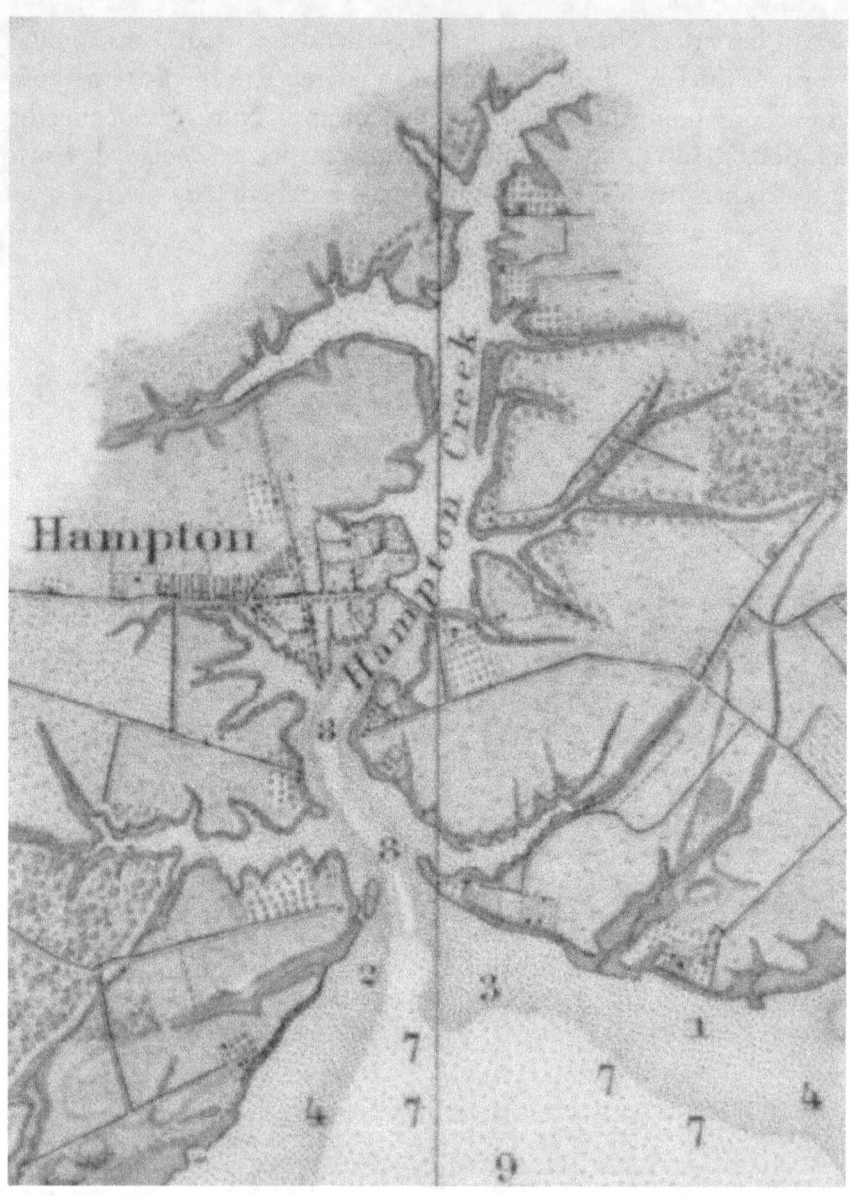

Captain Thomas Nuce began his work as a deputy in Kicotan (soon to be renamed "Elizabeth City," today called Hampton). Company policy forced some men to abandon their established homesteads on the east side of Southampton River (Hampton Creek on the map, now called Hampton River). Captain Nuce managed the vast Company Land and tenants on the east side of the river. [Map excerpt from,"Chesapeake Bay. York River Hampton Roads Chesapeake Entrance, Sheet No. 1," U.S. Coast Survey, 1863. Credit: NOAA's Historical Map & Chart Collection, www.historicalcharts.noaa.gov]

"The Burrough of Kiccowtan"

The Great Charter called for 3,000 acres to be "set out in the fields and territory" of each of the four boroughs or cities: Jamestown, Charles City, Henrico, and "the Burrough of Kiccowtan." These sets of 3,000 acres were to be called "the Company's land," and they were to be lived on and worked by the Company's tenants for half the profits. No doubt, the Company hoped that these vast tracts of land would inspire prospective investors and colonists. Land held the promise of profit. Each borough was also to have a reserve of the Company land to be used for the common stock of cattle. In addition to the Company land, each borough was to have 100 acres of Glebe land to generate income for the minister and several quantities of 1,500 acres to be known by the name of the borough or city. These lands would be used by the magistrates and officers of the city or borough to generate payment for their services.

The land policies of the Great Charter also called for the colony to allow a dwelling and four acres in any of the precincts for each artisan or tradesman who would ply his craft or trade from the house. The annual rent would be only four pence per year. (The average wage for a tradesman was about four pence per day.[47]) With this generous provision, the Company was endeavoring to encourage trades in the

---
[47] Kingsbury, *VCR-3*, 590.

colony and to discourage skilled workmen from dropping their trades for the seduction of tobacco profits.

The borough of Kiccowtan was renamed Elizabeth City about two years after the Great Charter was written, but people often continued to use the old name (in various spellings such as Kicotan, the one I will use).[48] Today, the original Elizabeth City is within the corporate limits of Hampton, Virginia. If we were to calculate the acreage in all of the land east of Hampton River and Harris Creek—encompassing all of Fox Hill, Buckroe Beach, Phoebus, Hampton University, and Hampton VA Hospital (but excluding Fort Monroe)—we would find about 6,200 acres, enough to account for the Great Charter's demands in Elizabeth City.

Before Deputy Captain Nuce arrived, Governor Yeardley had begun an assessment of which people could stay and which people would have to vacate the Company land, as the charter instructed. Company tenants could stay on the Company land. Any private person who was on the land as a result of a former governor's appointment could stay long enough to make recompense from the land for the houses built and for any land cleared. By November 11, 1619, Yeardley had apparently met with the people who didn't satisfy the criteria to stay, informing them that they could make their choice of a new home "along the bank of the great river between Kiquohtan & Newports Newes."[49]

Upon Captain Nuce's arrival in late 1620, Yeardley went to Elizabeth City to lend assistance and to persuade "the old Inhabitants here to remove from of this Land now chosen for the Company and to leave their houses with some reasonable consideration of help to build others upon their own dividents." Yeardley wrote to Sandys about this, calling it a "necessary trouble which at this time does possess me and suffer me to take a little more time therein."[50]

---

[48] While the Charter referred to the four areas as boroughs, the use of this administrative term did not survive. Kiccowtan was also spelled as Kiquotan, Kecoughtan, and Kicotan. Kicotan is one of the oldest spellings, and therefore, the one used most often in this account.

[49] Kingsbury, *VCR-3*, 227. (Incidentally, this is adequate documentation that the name "Newport News" had nothing to do with the Nuce family, a theory that is still bandied about on occasion.)

[50] Kingsbury, *VCR-3*, 123

We can only imagine the settlers' discontent. Some of the displaced men were Ancient Planters, having lived at Kicotan since the Third Supply or before. Several months after Nuce took charge of the Company land, William Capps petitioned the Company in London. Capps, along with William Tucker, had represented Kicotan as a burgess at the first General Assembly. Capps complained that his land was taken from him at the arrival of Captain Nuce because the land fell within the land now designated as Company Land. Capps's case was referred back to Virginia to be taken up by the next governor.[51]

Adam Dixon (a master caulker for ships and vessels) and William Kempe (who would be a burgess for Elizabeth City) both bypassed the Company and went straight to the king with their complaints. Dixon noted that Governor Argall had given him ground in Kicotan. Dixon and John Berry had built a house and cleared the ground. Governor Yeardley had turned them out "contrary to all equity justice or conscience to our great discomfort & other undoeinge." Kempe's petition spoke for William Julian, John Bush, Thomas Brewer, Thomas Willoby, John Gundry, and John Powell, each having found himself in similar circumstances as Dixon and Berry. The complaint was passed on to the Company, but the Company doubted Kempe's authority to speak for these men; still, the issue was sent forward to be addressed by the next governor.[52]

The Company had prioritized Elizabeth City for Deputy Nuce's work. He was to see that the Company tenants and his own tenants were placed, and he was to rid the land of the recalcitrant squatters. Nuce was in the weakened state of new arrivals, but in order to achieve the

---

[51] Kingsbury, *VCR-1*, 460–461.
[52] Martha W. McCartney, *Virginia Immigrants and Adventurers: A Biographical Dictionary, 1607-1635* (Baltimore: Genealogical Publishing Co., 2007), 440. Kingsbury, VCR-2, 44–45. Probably because of the colony's governmental collapse caused by the 1622 Indian attack, the cases weren't heard again until 1624. By that time, it seems everyone had an opinion about what to do for the displaced planters of Kicotan. Captain John Martin was advising them not to pay taxes until restitution was made to them. On January 3, 1624/25, Governor Wyatt and the council heard from William Julian, Sargeant Williams, and John Powell. Each of these men was given restitution in the form of tobacco, "wherewith he is well contented and satisfied which is the Company's desire" (H. R. McIlwaine, ed., *Minutes of the Counsel and General Court, 1622-1630, 1670-1676* (Richmond: Virginia State Library, 1924), 41 (hereafter: McIlwaine, Minutes).

Company's goals, it was necessary to push through. Given the strained situation, it is not surprising that Yeardley made himself immediately available to Nuce. With the newly arrived tenants and the aggressive resistance of old-timers, Elizabeth City was a tinderbox.

Also Happening in the Colony

If seating Company lands, placing Company tenants, creating a General Assembly, and investigating the former governor had been the only issues facing Governor Yeardley, perhaps he would have wanted a second term. However, a few more matters of importance fell to him.

These were turning-point years for Virginia. Generations of Virginia schoolchildren have learned that 1619 was a red-letter year because of four significant events: the General Assembly, the land policy, the arrival of the colony's first African people to Virginia, and the Company's plan to send marriageable maids to the colony. All four of these events would significantly alter the course of history across the colony in ways that are still studied to this very day.

The new land policies directly shaped the English founding of Virginia's Eastern Shore, and the bride plan would prove to have more of an influence than one might expect. No document has yet surfaced to suggest that the Africans' arrival to the colony directly affected the founding of a permanent English settlement on the other side of the bay. However, the arrival of African men and women in 1619 is of such significance to the nation's history that scholarly books and articles are still being written to help illuminate the importance of that day. However, for our purposes, we will view only the documentation of the first African people's arrival and only a snippet of information about the maids who came to marry Virginia colonists.

The arrival of the Africans was recorded by John Rolfe in a letter to Sir Edwin Sandys in January 1619/20. Rolfe was reporting about some happenings in the colony since Yeardley became governor. In his description of the August (1619) docking of a large Dutch man-of-war in the port of Point Comfort, Rolfe noted that the ship had "brought not any thing but 20. and odd Negroes, which the Governor and Cape Marchant bought for victualls [exchanged for food] (whereof he [the ship's captain] was in greate need as he pretended [asserted]) at the best and easyest rats [rates] they could."[53] That was the entirety of the disembarkation documentation about African people first coming ashore at Virginia. It is believed that at least half of these new arrivals were sent to be servants at Governor Yeardley's plantation and household and that the other half were disbursed as servants across five other settlements.[54] It is uncertain if the colony's first Africans were initially absorbed into Virginia's indentured labor system, or if their arrival as enslaved human beings immediately prompted some planters to keep them in slavery. Because colony officials paid for the Africans (food being the exchange), it may be that the Africans were considered to be Company laborers; however, no document has yet been found to clarify any decisions about their placement. Regarding the Eastern Shore, sixteen years would pass before records documented the arrival of African people. At that time, Alexander, Anthony, Sebastian, Polonia, Jane, Palatia, Cassanga, and John were listed as servants, but not enough information is present to know if any of these eight men and women had been among or were of any relation to the men and women who arrived in 1619.[55]

An outline of the Company's marriageable-maids project was reported in an account from the king's council for Virginia. This June 1620 report, "The State in Virginia," proclaimed that 100 women would

---

[53] Kingsbury, *VCR-3*, 243. Recent scholars have identified the ship as an English privateer, not a Dutch man-of-war.
[54] This theory is based on the 1623/24 muster that showed thirteen Negro servants in Yeardley's count and nine other Negro servants in five other places of the colony.
[55] Nugent, *Vol.* 1, 28. Northampton County, Court Book, No. 1, 52.

be sent to the colony to be wives for the tenants. According to Ransome, fifty-seven women were sent in the summer of 1621.[56] A year later, at a general court meeting in London on May 22, 1622, the Company approved a plan by the Adventurers who had funded the maids who were sent in the year before. These Adventurers asked for land to be laid out together because they intended to build a town called Maydes Towne. The Company approved the plan.[57]

Three years would pass until the records told of English women among the Eastern Shore settlers; at least two of these women are known to have arrived in the earliest maid shipments. One would marry John Blore.

---

[56] Ransome, David R. "Wives for Virginia, 1621." *The William and Mary Quarterly* 48, no. 1 (1991): 3-18. Accessed April 15, 2021. doi:10.2307/2937995.
[57] Kingsbury, *VCR-2*, 26. When the Company gave approval for Maids Town, they had not yet heard about the March 22, 1621/22 attack in Virginia. The plan for Maids Town was never realized.

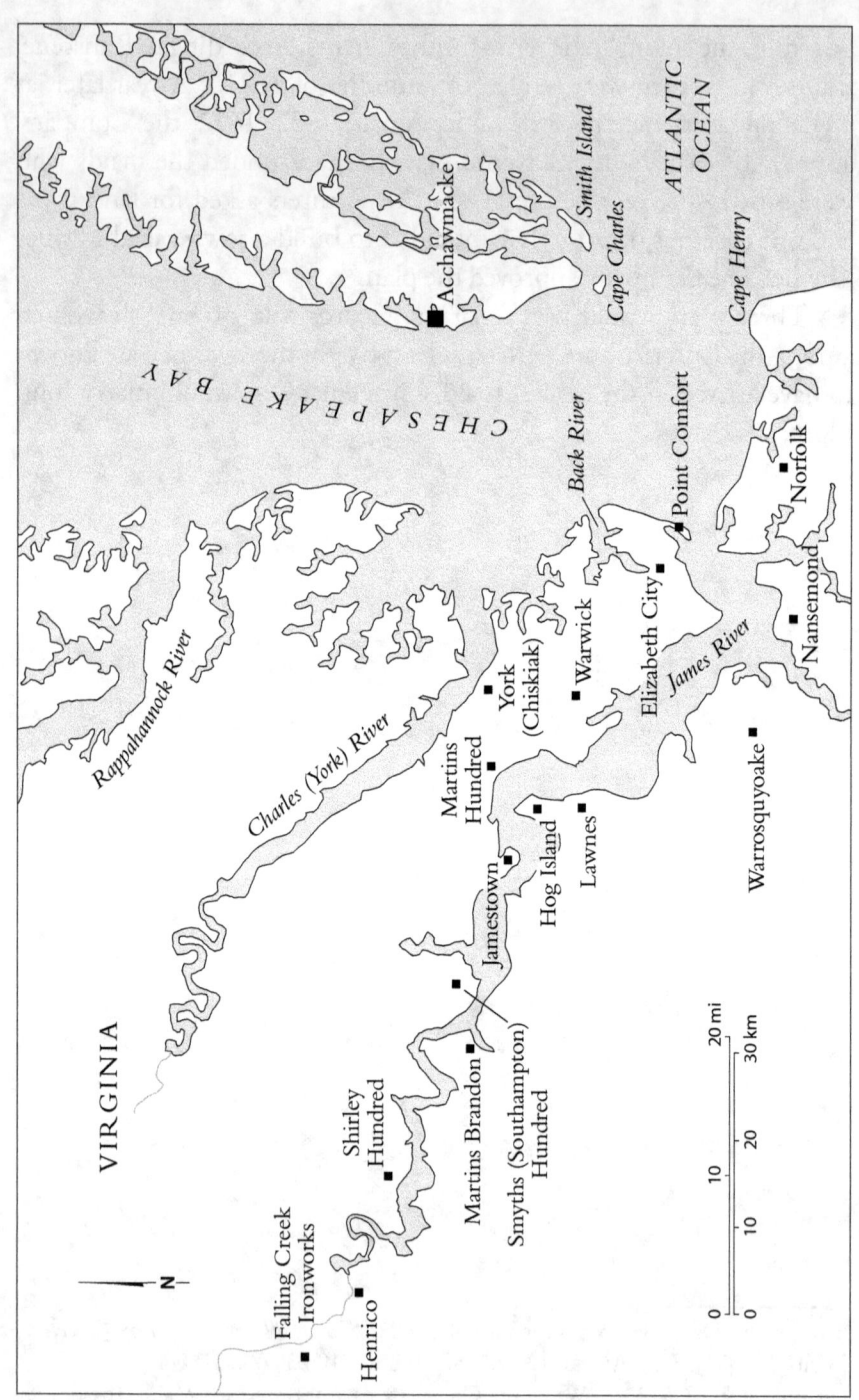

John Blore traveled no less than 100 miles by boat when he left Falling Creek Ironworks to settle on the Eastern Shore just south of Acchawmacke (Ackomack).

John and Frances Blore

Frances Lake arrived in the colony in late May of 1620, along with 199 other passengers on the 300-tun ship, the *London Marchant*.[58] Frances was twenty years old. The story of how this young woman met and decided to marry John Blore is lost, but the circumstances surrounding Blore at this particular time beg for a story to be told.

It is through John Blore that iron enters this narrative in an unexpected way. In the May 1620 broadside, iron topped the Company's list of desirable commodities. In these years, the Company hounded the Virginia colonists, imploring them to find resources for iron production. The near-frantic efforts to inspire the colonists to make iron had fallen flat in the presence of tobacco profits. Secretary Pory cited poor planning as the biggest stumbling block to iron; however, Pory also revealed that part of the problem was that the colony had no iron experts. In his June 12th (1620) letter to Sir Edwin Sandys, Pory noted that the Company had sent two German men "skillfull in mynes," but Pory claimed to

---

[58] Kingsbury *VCR-3*, 300–301; Vol. 1, 351. Frances's maiden name is taken from her will in which she named her siblings. Her will spelled the name as Lake and as Lacke (see Northampton County, *Court Book No. 2*, 61). A *tun* is a large cask capable of holding 252 gallons of liquid. A 300-tun ship would theoretically hold 300 such casks.

have a friend who was as skillful as the two Germans. He and this friend knew of a way to make iron with less labor and they were going to try it—"and yet will not goe about to prejudice the Iron mine neither."⁵⁹ (Pory's boast was never forthcoming of iron.) Almost a year later in May of 1621, Deputy George Thorpe wrote to Sir Edwin noting "in what a poore takinge wee are in for youer Iron works." Thorpe loaned the works "a man of my owne that hath buylt many Iron furnaces in England."⁶⁰ In July of 1621, John Rowe passed along a message to Sir Edwin, saying that "the Iron workes goeth forward veary well." Near that same time, the Company sent John Berkeley to oversee the advancement of the iron works, and Berkeley wrote back from Virginia that he expected to produce iron by the summer of 1622.⁶¹

All this to say that the site of Virginia's most promising iron works at that time appears to have been chosen sometime between the summer of 1619 (the dates of the General Assembly) and the next summer when Pory promised that his experiment would not prejudice the "iron mine." The site of this iron works, Falling Creek, was on John Blore's patent. (A patent was a land claim for which a person received an official grant.)

When the Great Charter allowed for grants of land based in part on a man's longevity, the procedures would have been hammered out in committee at the first General Assembly. John Blore, who came to Virginia in 1610, certainly qualified for a grant, and he had chosen 100 acres on Falling Creek, about seven miles upriver from Henrico. When Blore began clearing and planting his land, he no doubt discovered that the site had some promising features.

No record has been discovered that reveals Blore's Company career, but when we look at the four men known to have arrived with him in 1610, an interesting possibility emerges. Three of the men were associated with Elizabeth City. One (John Gundry) is known to have protested that Yeardley moved him off the land Argall had given him. Another, Miles Prickett, was one of the early salt makers for the colony.⁶²

Within the context of all that was happening, these meager facts raise the possibility that John Blore was also one of the men who had

---

⁵⁹ Kingsbury, *VCR-3*, 305.
⁶⁰ Kingsbury, *VCR-3*, 710–711.
⁶¹ Kingsbury, *VCR-3*, 464, 475–476, 640.
⁶² Kingsbury, *VCR-3*, 507.

been moved off of Elizabeth City Company Land. These facts also hint at the possibility that he could have been with Miles Prickett for the early salt-making operation.[63]

Let's imagine that Blore had finished his seven years with the Company in 1617 when Argall was governor, and that Blore was one of the men to whom Argall gave land in Kicotan (later called Elizabeth City). Then in 1619, Yeardley arrived with instructions to unseat any men on the newly appointed Company Land who were not current Company tenants. Perhaps Blore merely took in his crop, packed and left. He didn't just go across the river at Elizabeth City, he went as far away as allowed to that date, up the river from Henrico, the colony's most remote city.

As a Company tenant, probably a laborer with broad experience, Blore would have recognized the features of a good site for iron production: running water, hardwood trees, ore, and close, navigable water. Perhaps after thoroughly exploring his 100 acres and discovering the features, Blore saw an opportunity to make a trade for his own profit, or maybe he was one of the many men who truly championed the possibilities of Virginia. Whatever the case may have been, the site was deemed excellent for iron working, and due to the Company's dogged persistence, no time was wasted.

Before giving up the site for the good of the colony, Blore would have harvested any crop he had planted; he may have even worked for hire, helping to prepare the site for the iron works. He was young, probably healthy, and he was a free man. Although he could have worked longer for the Company, he wanted his own plantation. What's more, he had recently met his future wife. John Blore could now more than dream of having a family.

We know about Blore's first patent because of a 1625 land record that revealed his surrender of the 100-acre patent "for the use of the Iron Works." That land was on the southerly side of the James River below present-day Richmond. Several pages later, the record revealed the land

---

[63] Dr. Ames was also of the opinion that John Blower had been one of Lieutenant Cradock's seventeen men at Smith Island, and that he was "one of the earliest permanent settlers on the Eastern Shore" (Susie M. Ames, *The Virginia Eastern Shore in the 17th Century* (New York, Russell & Russell, 1973 [original copyright 1940]), 21).

that Blore took to replace his first patent. This new patent consisted of 140 acres on the Eastern Shore.[64]

No documentation exists to describe the details of the negotiation that brought about Blore's surrender of his patent at Falling Creek. Surely he expected due compensation for any work he had done. By unknown means, he received an extra forty acres in the exchange; if that forty acres was indeed part of the negotiation, it was unusual. However, Blore's situation appears to have been unusual.

Imagine again, if you will, that Blore had been one of the displaced planters at Elizabeth City, and then he was again displaced at Falling Creek. At Elizabeth City, he had complied with the request to move, an action that would have engendered more sympathy toward him the second time around. Yeardley would have felt gratitude toward such a man; he would have wanted to do right by Blore.

Now let's stretch our imaginations a bit further. The Company's broadside was made public about the time that Frances Lake arrived and about the same time that Blore would have been in negotiations with Yeardley for a new patent. If indeed Blore had been a salt man with Miles Prickett, Yeardley might have broached the subject of the Eastern Shore or Blore might have been the one to suggest it to Yeardley. In conversations at a local James City ordinary, Blore may have conversed with Secretary Pory; indeed, Blore may even have been one of the men Pory said chortled at the Company's plan to give fifty acres each to salt workers on Smith Island. Perhaps Frances Lake was present during such a conversation and asked to know more. Perhaps she became enamored of the Eastern Shore right along with Pory.

Chances are good that John Blore and Frances Lake met shortly after her arrival in late May of 1620. He was only two years older than she, but he had more seniority in the colony than most other bachelors, a fact that surely gave him precedence in meeting available maidens and a feature that made him an attractive suitor. It isn't entirely clear if Frances had been sent as part of the Company's plan to supply "brides" to the colony; however, the records never showed her as anyone's head right. This absence means that she probably was sent as a prospective bride,

---

[64] Kingsbury, *VCR-4*, 552, 559. Blore's name was spelled as Blower in this early record. I have used Blore, a later spelling from the Northampton County court records; however, it should be noted that Blower was a commonly used spelling of the name.

because a Company caveat provided that "no man marrying these weomen [should] expect the proportion of Land useually alotted for every head."[65]

The records are silent about John and Frances's marriage date. They are also silent as to when they went to the Eastern Shore to seat Blore's plantation. When the Blores made their home on the Eastern Shore, they most likely had the help of one or two young servants, but—and this is purely speculative—it's possible that at least one other couple may have joined them. Imagine a lone, young couple grappling to survive in a place separated from others by twenty miles of that ocean-like bay. Enlisting another of the "brides" and her new husband to take on the challenge would have been a practical thing to do. The records are silent about this also, although the 1624 muster shows at least one other of the "brides" and her husband then living on the Eastern Shore.[66]

All the components that worked together to put the Blores on the Eastern Shore would have taken place within a span of months, including Thomas Nuce's arrival to begin work on the crisis at Elizabeth City. As noted earlier, on his voyage to Virginia, Deputy Nuce was accompanied by John Wilcocks. Here was another man who was in the right place at the right time.

---

[65] Kingsbury, *VCR-3*, 494.
[66] John Camden Hotten, ed., *The Original Lists of Persons of Quality: Emigrants, Religious, Exiles, Political Rebels, Serving Men Sold for a Term of Years, Apprentices, Children Stolen, Maidens Pressed, And Others, Who Went From Great Britain to the American Plantations, 1600–1700* (London: Empire State Book Co, 1874), 188–189. Jennifer Potter, *The Jamestown Brides* (London: Atlantic Books, 2018), 261–263.

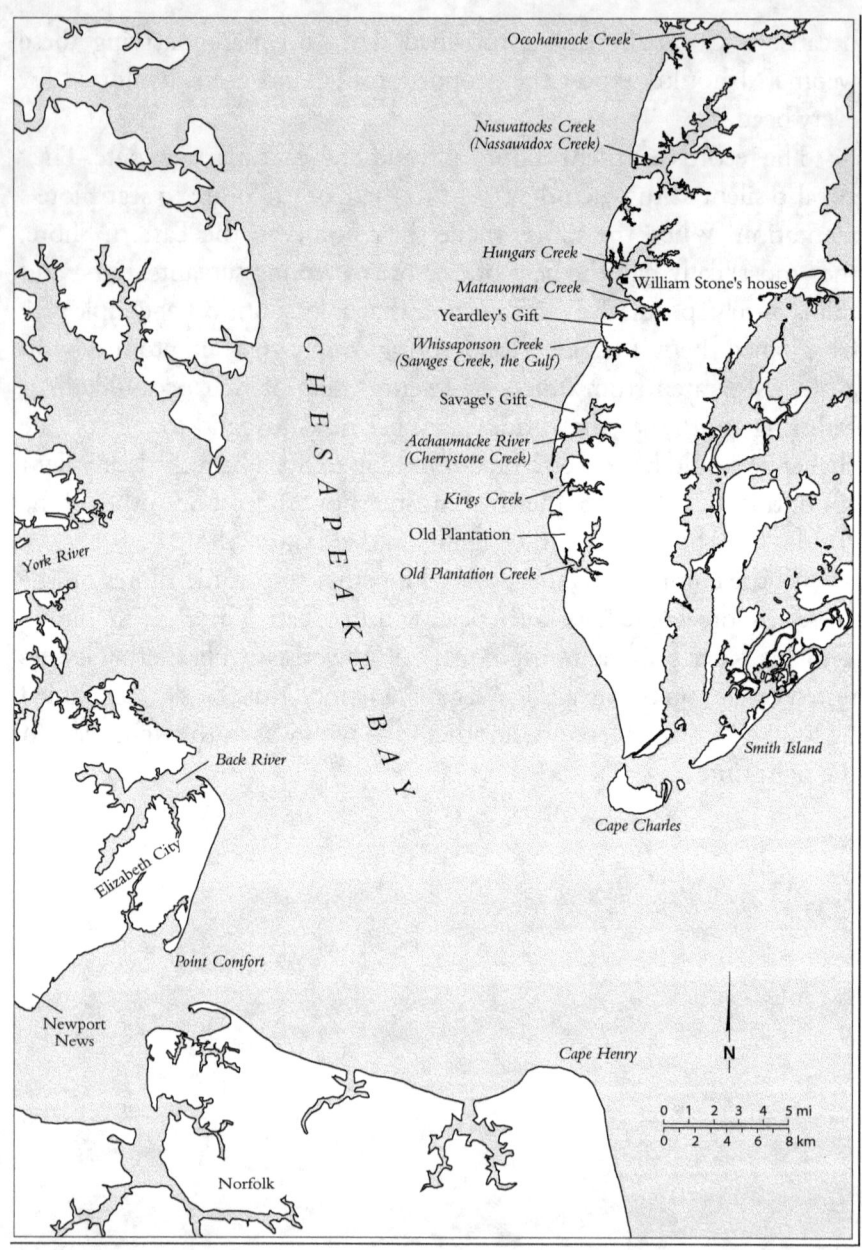

Smith Island was the site of the early salt works. The Blores settled at *Old Plantation*. During most of the first two decades of Eastern Shore settlement, the northern boundary was at *Mattawoman Creek*. William Stone was the first person to build a house north of that boundary in c. 1638.

John Wilcocks

John Wilcocks of Plymouth came to Virginia in 1620 on the Company's ship, the *Bona Nova*.[67] The *Bona Nova* and her pinnace had left the Downs on September 7th to arrive in Virginia by mid-to-late October.[68]

This crossing also brought Deputy Thomas Nuce with his commission to manage the Company lands. Had Wilcox and Nuce known one another before this journey, or did they become acquainted during their many weeks at sea? Either way, we know that they formed a trusting relationship; when Wilcocks wrote his will two years later, he named Nuce as a probate overseer.[69] Trust doesn't get much stronger than that.

Governor Yeardley would have brought Captain Nuce up-to-date on the Elizabeth City situation as soon as possible after the *Bona Nova* anchored off Point Comfort. If by that time Wilcocks had indeed

---

[67] Martha W. McCartney, *Virginia Immigrants and Adventurers: A Biographical Dictionary, 1607-1635* (Baltimore: Genealogical Publishing Co., 2007), 745.
John Frederick Dorman, *Adventures of Purse and Person, Virginia, 1607-1624/5: Families A-F*, (Baltimore: Genealogical Publishing Company, 2004), 69.
[68] Kingsbury, *VCR-3*, 406. While it is known that Wilcocks came on the Bona Nova in 1620, it is possible that he came earlier in the year; however, only this one voyage of the Bona Nova in 1620 was found in the records.
[69] nationalarchives.gov.uk

become a confidant, Nuce would have pulled him into the discussions. Upon seeing Elizabeth City's disorder firsthand and hearing the verbal abuse of those who weren't quietly leaving the Company Land, perhaps Wilcocks looked for ways that he might be of service.

All of the new people, including Nuce and Wilcocks, were unseasoned to living in Virginia. The arduous ocean journey often left newcomers weak and susceptible to diseases. Food was usually in short supply, and most people had been accustomed to drinking ale or beer, certainly not the local water. (Nuce would find the water so poor that he built a brick-lined well in an attempt to improve it.[70]) Seasoning took at least six months. The Virginians encouraged the Company to give new people time to adjust before expecting them to work, and the Company encouraged the Virginians to build guest houses in each borough to accommodate at least fifty newly arrived people. Neither group listened well to the other, and newcomers suffered for it. If people didn't have time to season, they often died. Yeardley's thorny problem had become a hornet's nest with the increasing number of new, unseasoned colonists arriving in the colony.

In the previous chapter, a case was made for John and Frances Blore as the first Eastern Shore settlers. In that sequence of events, John met Frances in the summer of 1620 soon after her arrival; they married and were on the Eastern Shore by late fall of that same year. In such a scenario, it's possible that Nuce and Wilcocks accompanied Yeardley to see that the Blores (and others who may have joined them) were safely settled on Blore's 140-acre patent. Yeardley no doubt would have taken the opportunity to view Smith Island, considering that the Company's broadside of the previous May had laid out a questionable strategy for reopening the saltworks there.

No letters—if they exist—have yet surfaced to shed light on how Wilcocks came to seat a plantation on the Eastern Shore. Some writers have said that George Yeardley laid out Company land at Ackomack River (Cherrystone Inlet), placed a contingent of Company tenants there, and appointed Wilcocks as the commander. My analysis of the records reveals the same picture but with a different caption.

Imagine this: Since the time of the broadside, talk over pints of ale at Jamestown had turned to the Company's ridiculous plan for "Smiths

---

[70] McCartney, *Virginia Immigrants*, 519.

Iland." Blore heard about it around the time he gave up his land at Falling Creek and asked Yeardley about the possibility of land on the Eastern Shore. The governor gave Blore the go-ahead. Soon after, Governor Yeardley and Deputy Nuce weighed and measured every scheme they could imagine for relieving the misery of inadequate shelter and limited sustenance in Elizabeth City. Deputy Nuce, newly responsible for the Company Land and its tenants, felt the weight of his task and often talked to his trusted friend Wilcocks about the wretched conditions suffered by the new tenants. Nuce's wife, Anne, had also come to Virginia, but she was "great with child," and Nuce didn't want to worry her more than was necessary. (In late May of 1621, Nuce happily reported that his wife had just added a "jolly boy" to the colony.[71])

In the discussions, Wilcocks offered to seat a plantation if he could have some of the Company tenants. Why couldn't Wilcocks merely command a contingent of tenants on the Elizabeth City Company land? He could, but Yeardley saw an opportunity here. Wilcocks didn't have the means yet to obtain his own patent or his own servants, but what if they considered the Eastern Shore a precinct of Elizabeth City? What if the governor allowed Wilcocks to lease land at the Eastern Shore, just as men did on the west side of Elizabeth City's Southampton River? And, instead of owning servants, what if he could hire some of the Company tenants who needed placement? Hiring them—rather than just using them—would sidestep potential perceptions of impropriety. Once Wilcocks had obtained the means to import his own servants, the Company tenants would be released to work Company land when Deputy Nuce could get around to addressing the other Company lands.

Whether it happened this way or a similar way, it was a brilliant plan. By taking tenants to the Eastern Shore, some of Elizabeth City's chaos was relieved. It also bolstered settlement on that side of the water. Blore's situation had provided a convenient stepping stone, and now Secretary Pory was considering the Eastern Shore for the 500 acres assigned to the Secretary's office. (He would wait to make his decision when he actually saw some tenants step off the boat.) The idea of re-opening the "Smith Iland" saltworks continued to draw the leadership's attention to the Eastern Shore.

---

[71] Kingsbury, *VCR-3*, 458.

Upon seeing the fresh, essentially unspoiled land of the Eastern Shore, Wilcocks may have been as smitten as Pory to the idea of planting there. Perhaps the idea of hiring tenants may have been based on opening the saltworks, and that Wilcocks would release the tenants when the salt operation was ready to go. Being at Wilcocks's plantation, the men would gain experience living in an isolated setting. (Just over a year later, the Virginia Council would write that living on the Eastern Shore was "a matter very Considerable, since that place ys [is] soe farr from James Cyttie."[72])

Once the decision was made, Wilcocks would have wanted to get a crop into the ground as early as possible. Because of seasoning, he and any servants and tenants who came to Virginia in the same voyage probably wouldn't have been fit for strenuous work until April of 1621. This may be a reason why Wilcocks chose the site of his plantation on a neck off Ackomack River where old fields—cleared from years of usage by the native people—were numerous.

Whatever the actual course of events, Wilcocks had a plantation on the Eastern Shore by the fall of 1621 when John Pory sailed across the bay to place the Secretary's tenants on the 500 acres he had chosen—upon Yeardley's advice—as the Secretary's Land.[73] Pory observed the following:

> Having but ten men meanly provided to plant the Secretaries land on the Easterne shore neere Acomack (Captain Wilcocks plantation, the better to secure and assist each other). Sir George Yearley intending to visit Smiths Iles, fell so sicke that he could not, so that he sent me with Estinien Moll, a French-man, to finde a convenient place to make salt in....Having taken a muster of the companies tenants, I went to Smiths Iles, where was our Salt-house: not farre off wee found a more convenient place, and so returned to James towne.[74]

---

[72] Kingsbury, *VCR-3*, 585.
[73] McIlwaine, *Minutes*, 148.
[74] John Smith, *Generall Historie*, 274. By saying that ten men were "meanly" provided, Pory tells us that he was not sent the twenty men that were promised. In this sense, "meanly" implies a meaning such as "cheaply."

The Secretary's Land would also have included old, cleared fields. Influential Company men had expressed a preference for such fields, but firsthand experience told that such land was "the barrenest of places" being "generaly worne out & ungrateful to the planters."[75] Still, old fields rimmed by woods held a promise of quick work for building shelter and for getting a crop into the ground.

Soon after his first voyage to the Eastern Shore, Pory took a second voyage across the bay to the Eastern Shore and up the bay to the Patuxent River (now in Maryland). In his notes, he said that they "returned the same way wee came, to the laughing Kings on the Easterne shore." Thomas Savage accompanied Pory on both of these voyages. Pory remarked that Savage, "with much honestie and good successe hath served the publike without any publike recompence."[76] When Pory and his party returned to Jamestown after a few weeks, the government had been passed to Sir Francis Wyatt. The date for that transfer was set by the Company to take place on November 18, 1621.[77]

Some writers have pointed to Pory's muster of the Company's tenants as evidence that Wilcocks was commanding Company Land and Company tenants. An alternate explanation is found in a directive from the Company written on July 24, 1621, to instruct the new governor, Sir Francis Wyatt, as he prepared to leave for Virginia. One of Wyatt's orders was to place tenants on the lands belonging to the various offices. This expectation had been neglected by current officers and some tenants had been hired out. Wyatt directed that from now on officers were not permitted to hire out their tenants.[78]

Having read that directive, Yeardley would have prepared to answer any questions about who was where when the new governor arrived. When Yeardley became too ill to make the trip to the Eastern Shore, he gave Pory instructions to take a muster of the Company tenants.

In the July 24th orders for the governor-elect, the Company included some commendations to the colony. Among them was one that reflects an awakening to the promises of places like the Eastern Shore:

---

[75] Kingsbury, *VCR-4*, 107. This observation was made by George Sandys in a letter to John Ferrar, dated April 8, 1623.
[76] John Smith, *Generall Historie*, 276.
[77] Kingsbury, *VCR-3*, 471.
[78] Kingsbury, *VCR-3*, 475, 479.

"The voyages and discoveries already made within the land, as also upon the Sea Coast, we highly Comend; and desire a constant course be held therein, for in that consists the very life of the plantation."[79]

---

[79] Kingsbury, *VCR-3*, 479, 488.

Thomas Savage, Dales Gift, and Lady Dale's People

Readers who are acquainted with even a smattering of Eastern Shore history know that Thomas Savage is credited with being the first Eastern Shore colonist. It's certainly still a possibility that Savage was the first, but it's just as certain a possibility that Blore was the first, or even John Wilcocks. These men were not racing to be the first, so any current debate is really of no importance. Nevertheless, Thomas Savage is recognized, as he should be, as a man of great consequence; after all, he was the first Eastern Shore colonist to have a well-documented, surviving line of descendants.

First or not, Thomas Savage's career as an interpreter and trader tremendously influenced settlement on Virginia's Eastern Shore. His life is the subject of books and the stuff of legend, but for our purposes it's important to know that he, as the interpreter on a number of commissions over the bay, was responsible for opening trade with the native people of the Eastern Shore.

Savage had gone with Captain Samuel Argall in 1614 at the behest of Deputy Governor Dale to negotiate for land from which the English colonists could operate their salt and fishing camps. The land that the native leader gave over at that time was dubbed "Dales Gift," but the land was for the Company, not for Dale personally.[80] Pory noted this when he wrote about the land "which Sir Thomas Dale bought from the Indyans for the company."[81]

From 1614 onward, no one recorded the boundaries of the land that was procured in Dale's name. In the 1625 list of patents, no patent to Dale was noted on the Eastern Shore. It wasn't until 1628 that "rumors" about the land were officially questioned.

The questions came when Charles Harmar asked to have 100 acres outside of Old Plantation Creek. This creek had been a boundary of the Eastern Shore settlement up to that time. The General Court in James City considered Harmar's request on December 8, 1628 and noted:

> "there hath beene an uncertaine Rumor of a greate quantity of land there or neere unto the same belonging unto the Lady Dale But Considering that for as much as there remaineth heere noe certaine knowledge thereof eyther uppon Record or otherwise, and deeming it unreasonable and unlikely that soe greate a tract of Land as from Cape Charles thither should belong to any particuler divident...."

The General Court permitted Harmar to have the 100 acres in the new territory as long as no evidence was brought forward to prove that it belonged to Lady Dale.[82] (No one ever came forward to claim that she owned the land as had been rumored.)

Sir Thomas Dale had died in 1619 and his will was probated in the following January. His widow, Lady Elizabeth Dale, inherited her husband's "plate money, household stuff, goods and chattels whatsoever."[83] It appears that Dale had not claimed any land in Virginia, and the only land perhaps credited to him was a small tract near Goose

---

[80] Alexander Brown, *The First Republic in America* (Boston & New York: Houghton, Mifflin & Co.,1898), 420.
Edward D. Neill, *History of the Virginia Company of London* (Albany, N.Y.: J. Munsell, 1869), 111. Most likely, trade with the Indians had been taking place since Savage first visited the Shore with Captain Argall in 1614, but Martin and Savage did not formalize the trade relationship until after 1619 under Governor Yeardley's direction.
[81] Kingsbury, *VCR-3*, 303.
[82] McIlwaine, *Minutes*, 179. Harmar had been an overseer of Lady Dale's cattlemen.
[83] NEHGS. The New England Historical and Genealogical Register, Volume 47, 1893. N.p.: Heritage Books, 2016, 403.

Hill on Jamestown Island.[84] This may be where his Virginia cattle were left in the care of an overseer whose name was Colfer.[85] After receiving the estate, Lady Dale took a great interest in Virginia investments, although she never lived there. On June 11, 1621, the Virginia Company recorded that Lady Dale, the widow of Sir Thomas Dale, "desired a Patent for a particular Plantation." It granted her request and sent instructions to Governor Yeardley to allot the land to her.[86] The "particular Plantation" was not identified.

After the Indian attack of 1622, the Virginia governor and council found themselves in the position of having to defend their decisions for "quitting of soe many Plantations" for the purpose of bringing people into safer, protected places such as Jamestown. In a January 1622/23 letter to the Company, the Virginia Council chose one case to serve as an example of why the "quitting" of plantations was necessary at this chaotic time. It was the case of Lady Dale.

> A muster taken of my Lady dales family, which consisted of two and twentie wherof eight were boys, most of the men were new and untrayned with very little munitione, and but six peeces and one Armour amongst them, and 54 headd of Cattle, which all those men were nott Sufficyent to guarde, except eyther the place or Industry of inclosure had given advantage.[87]

In other words, these fourteen men, eight boys, and their fifty-four cattle would likely have been killed in an isolated, unfortified settlement. The implication is that Lady Dale's people were relocated from her plantation. Given that the officials in London did not grant a plantation to Lady Dale until June of 1621, it's likely that her people were never placed on her plantation. None of Lady Dale's people were listed among the dead after the attack, a fact that supports the likelihood that they had not yet been placed.[88]

---

[84] McIlwaine, *Minutes*, 192.
[85] McIlwaine, *Minutes*, 48. The succession of Lady Dale's overseers in this first decade appears to have been Colfer, Henry Watkins, Charles Harmar, and William Hamby.
[86] Kingsbury, *VCR-1*, 491–492.
[87] Kingsbury, *VCR-4*, 12.
[88] From England on May 20, 1622, Lady Dale complained that "her people in Virginia doe not performe covenants with her according to their Contracts" (Kingsbury, Vol. 2, 14). When this was written, another month would pass before word of the attack reached England.

It appears that Lady Dale's crew and cattle arrived during the colony's chaotic months soon after the attack and were never sent to inhabit her new plantation (the unidentified 500 acres).[89] In discussions about what to do with them, most likely someone would have mentioned Dales Gift; indeed, this may be when that "uncertain Rumor" began to take shape. It seems that no one knew for certain if the land was actually Dale's or even how much land was involved, but at this particular time, amid the chaos, those details were the least of anyone's concern. The decision was made to transport Lady Dale's people and cattle to the Eastern Shore.

When Lady Dale died nineteen years later in 1641, she bequeathed land in Charles Hundred and Sherlie Hundred, and 500 unspecified acres in Virginia.[90] It wasn't until four years after her death that her executors applied for a 1,000-acre grant in the name of Lady Dale, the land "due unto her as being the sole Executrix of Sir Thomas Dale to whom it was due by bill of adventure into this colony."[91] It was a brilliant piece of legal work—probably inspired by the old rumor and by very clever assignees—but it was not linked to the old Company land called Dales Gift. By that time, Dales Gift—at least the most southern part of it—had been absorbed into a multitude of patents.

---

[89] Kingsbury, *VCR-3*, 643.
[90] Northampton County, Va., *Court Book No. 2*, 36.
[91] Nugent, *Vol. 1*, 163.

Thomas Savage and George Yeardley

I magine that you are Sir Thomas Dale in 1614, sending your most trusted deputies and interpreter to negotiate with the Eastern Shore native werowance, a man who has proven to be friendly toward Englishmen. You want land for making salt from the ocean water and for sheltering the salters and the fishermen. Would you command your agents to ask for a small sliver of land at the southern point of the Eastern Shore, or would you ask for as much land as you could get?

Now imagine that you are the great werowance, a man averse to warring, but loving "husbandry and hunting."[92] What decision would you make about a dividing line? What natural features of the Eastern Shore would you choose for that boundary?

I might choose the great inlet known today as Cherrystone. In the early years, it was known as Ackomack River.

When John Smith visited the Eastern Shore in 1608, he found the local werowance at Ackomack. Thirteen years later, when John Pory visited in late 1621, he found the werowance at Occohannock. By this time, the English were in a protective relationship with the Eastern

---

[92] Smith, *Generall Historie*, 276.

Shore Indians (whom Pory called "the laughing Kings"). Pory noted that diverse nations would invade these Indians "were they not protected by us."[93]

Who had achieved this relationship? Had it been Dale, Yeardley, or both at separate times? Whatever the case may have been, Thomas Savage was no doubt essential to the alliance.

As we saw in Chapter 3, Yeardley had been a right-hand man to Dale. If Dale could have spared him to be away from Bermuda Hundred, chances are good that Yeardley was a part of the mission to negotiate land for the first saltworks. If so, he would have been privy to the conversation with the werowance and he would have seen Thomas Savage's skills first hand.

When Yeardley returned to Virginia as governor in January of 1618/19, one of his first acts was to employ Thomas Savage as an interpreter for public business. Savage was then living at Captain John Martin's plantation on the south bank of the James River. After completion of that business, Savage returned to live at Martin's, but Yeardley had need of him again. After the second matter was completed, Yeardley didn't send Savage back. This didn't sit well with Captain Martin who said that Savage was his servant and he needed him "to go abroad in his shallop."[94]

Besides learning that Thomas Savage resided at Martin's plantation in 1619, it's clear that Yeardley had great confidence in Savage's skill and that the two men spent a fair amount of time together during Yeardley's governorship. In the complaint made by Captain John Martin about Yeardley's use of Savage, Yeardley replied that he had not known Savage was Martin's or anyone's servant; in fact, he had thought Savage was "a public interpreter." By the time Yeardley answered Martin's complaints in February 1624/25, Thomas Savage was married and living on the Eastern Shore among fifty other settlers.[95]

It wasn't until 1668 that the records provided a bit of information that could be paired with another bit of information from 1635 to reveal an extraordinary event that occurred in the years of Yeardley's first governorship or very soon after. That event was a meeting during which

---

[93] Smith, *Generall Historie*, 277.
[94] Kingsbury, *VCR-4*, 514.
[95] Dorman, *Adventures of Purse and Person*, 69.

the Eastern Shore werowance released a large tract of land to Thomas Savage and a large tract of land to George Yeardley.[96] No record reveals when these grants were given, nor whether they were bestowed at the same time or as separate events. If we wish to make a reasoned guess, it's necessary to look at the context of the day.

John Blore had moved from Falling Creek and settled on Old Plantation Creek. With Elizabeth City in flux, Deputy Nuce's friend John Wilcocks established a plantation on the Eastern Shore; for certain, he was there in the fall of 1621 when Secretary Pory set ten tenants near Wilcock's plantation called Ackomack. Who had paved the way with the native people for these first men to live on the Eastern Shore?

Yeardley's responses to the complaints of Captain Martin show that Yeardley viewed and used Ensign Thomas Savage as a public interpreter. Not enough information is present to draw an inference about whether or not Yeardley and Savage traveled together or whether Yeardley assigned Savage to carry out some tasks independently.

People have made their guesses over the years and mine is that Yeardley and Savage were together when the Eastern Shore werowance released those tracts of land. Yeardley, as we've heard, liked to dot his i's and cross his t's, and this was an important task, one he'd personally want to lead. The grants probably hadn't been given before Secretary Pory placed his ten people in the fall of 1621, or he would likely have mentioned it. As it were, Pory characterized Thomas Savage as having served without any public recompense.[97] (Later, his grant was characterized as his divident, which is a form of public recompense.[98])

---

[96] Nugent, *Vol. 1*, 30, 75. Howard Mackey and Marlene A. Groves, *Northampton County, Virginia, Record Book: Court Cases, Vol. 9, 1664-1674* (Rockport, ME: Picton Press, 2003), 152–153.

[97] Smith, *Generall Historie*, 276. Dr. Ames also noted that Thomas Savage's land at Savage's Neck was probably allowed to him as a reward for his service (see Susie M. Ames, *The Virginia Eastern Shore in the 17th Century* (New York, Russell & Russell, 1973 [original copyright 1940]), 20).

[98] The early records show that planters were required to purchase land from the native people before claiming it as their own. The negotiation was usually between the planter and the werowance. After clearing the ownership through the native people, the planter then acquired the English government's sanction for the land. That Savage's land was later called his "divident" means that it was recognized as his rightful land based on service and/or headrights. (Personal investment [adventure] stock was also recognized for land grants, but no record shows that Savage owned Company stock.)

If the werowance's gifts weren't given before Pory's visit, when were they given? I submit that the meeting took place after the 1622 Indian attack when Yeardley was sent by Governor Wyatt to assess the Eastern Shore for the purpose of beginning a plantation there for three to four hundred colonists.[99] Under such a directive, Yeardley and Savage would surely have met with the werowance to clear the way for this major undertaking. These Englishmen would have explained the disorder and crowded conditions on the mainland, and this particular werowance would have listened with uncommon compassion. Not only would this werowance have approved of the proposal, he would have wanted to convey to these men, particularly to Savage whom he called "my son," his deep feelings of love. What better way to express his affection than to give each of them a great tract of land?

While no record has been found that describes the sequence of events, I propose that this is when the Eastern Shore native people fully abandoned all land on the peninsula south of a creek called Mattawomes, the northern boundary to Yeardley's grant.

Chaos had ensued after the attack, including a devastating summer sickness. Some storytellers portrayed Yeardley's visit to the Eastern Shore at that time as an idyllic sail, a vacation to explore his land; however, the Company records reveal that his assignment was the opposite of idyllic and resulted in threats of treason. Additionally, I suggest to you that Yeardley owned no land on the Eastern Shore prior to that assignment.

The story of Yeardley's expedition at the behest of Governor Wyatt is well worth knowing, not only for what it may tell about Eastern Shore history but for what it reveals about the Virginia Company's leadership during that fragile time. It's a story for another day. For now, let's tie up a few loose threads.

---

[99] Kingsbury, *VCR-3*, 656–657.

A Few Loose Threads

First Settlers

Two parties are candidates for identification as the first permanent settlers on Virginia's Eastern Shore: John Wilcocks and the Blores. It's well-known that Wilcocks's plantation preceded John Pory's visit in the late fall of 1621. John and Frances Blore's presence on the Eastern Shore was first documented in the 1623/24 muster.

This book puts forward the premise that John and Frances Blore were the first permanent settlers on the Eastern Shore. Why would I say the Blores preceded Wilcocks whose early presence is irrefutable? We are fortunate to have Pory's words about Wilcocks's presence; however, the absence of any mention of the Blores cannot be said to rule out their presence. The aggregate of facts, as presented in this book, shows that the Blores likely preceded Wilcocks (though probably not by much).

Thomas Savage was not the first settler on the Eastern Shore, but his work was essential to creating the three settlements (the Blores, Wilcocks, Pory's tenants) that effectually became one settlement. While Savage didn't have a "permanent" residence on the Eastern Shore prior to 1622, the local werowance considered him "family" because of the trade relationship they nurtured together; this unique bond puts Thomas Savage in a category all his own.

Laughing Kings

You may have noticed that I did not name the werowance. Because this subject has become fairly complex over the centuries, I will merely say for now that he was known as "the Laughing King." Just as the English called Powhatan by the name of his tribe, the Laughing King was called after the name of his tribe. "Laughing Kings" wasn't the correct pronunciation; it was what an inexperienced, colonial English ear heard. The malapropism was too catchy not to repeat. For those of you with knowledge of Eastern Shore history, note that "Gingaskin" has a derivation that includes the word "king." That's part of the picture, and it—including the werowance's name—is a subject for another day.

Captain Wilcocks

In the 1624/25 Eastern Shore muster, Wilcocks was one of seven men who owned armor. Other than Commander Epps who owned six, Wilcocks owned four, Savage owned three, and John Howe owned two. Perregrim Watkins, Robert Ball, and John Blore each owned one. While ownership of armor is not a sure sign that a man was or had been a soldier, it seems to be a good indicator.

It's probable that Wilcocks came to Virginia with the title of "Captain," meaning that he had likely been a soldier. When he was called to arms to fight the Indians, he apparently didn't hesitate but prepared to die, as evidenced by the will he wrote at that time. The will reveals that his wife in England was the mother of a daughter (Wilcocks's stepdaughter) who was old enough to be an executrix. While this tells us nothing about Wilcocks's age, it suggests that his wife may have been at least in her mid-thirties. It follows that Wilcocks was old enough to have earned the rank of Captain as a soldier.

Elizabeth City

For a number of years—at least through to the time of the February 1624/25 muster—the Eastern Shore settlement was considered a part of Elizabeth City. This detail isn't a feature of the current story except to suggest that the connection between these two places resulted from Deputy Thomas Nuce's friendship with John Wilcocks. By 1623/24, the Eastern Shore and Elizabeth City each had their own representatives in the General Assembly, but the 1624/25 muster identified the Eastern Shore as still a part of the Elizabeth City corporation.

This early symbiotic relationship between the two places came about in great part because settlers who went to the Eastern Shore often came directly from Elizabeth City. It's indicated later in that decade that a few colonists had residences in both places. With that in mind, it's easy to imagine that progress on the Eastern Shore was sometimes modeled on growth in Elizabeth City. Specifically, the first Ackomack church may have been fashioned after the second Elizabeth City church. (The Elizabeth City church was built circa 1624, and the Ackomack church was probably built within a few years after that.) The site of Ackomack's first church has not yet been discovered, but it's believed to have been on the Secretary's Land, near the mouth of Kings Creek. The Ackomack church had a graveyard, and burials were also allowed in the chancel.[100] This church stood for a number of years, as did the second church at Elizabeth City.[101]

Old Plantation

Blore's plantation was at the south end of today's Old Plantation Neck. This neck's southern border is the creek known as Old Plantation Creek. This name, Old Plantation, has perplexed many writers over the years.

Anne Floyd Upshur and Ralph T. Whitelaw, the creators of the Eastern Shore's most-used tome of local history, Virginia's Eastern Shore, addressed this issue in an article they contributed to the Virginia Magazine of History and Biography in 1942. "Historians have generally assumed that it [Dales Gift] must have been located somewhere on Old Plantation Creek, and this premise was accepted as accounting for the name given to that creek."[102] In this article, Upshur and Whitelaw addressed the location of Dales Gift, and they also addressed the origin of the name "Old Plantation." They ruled out that Dales Gift

---

[100] Northampton County, Va., *Court Book No. 1, 1632–1640*, 129. Commander John Howe was buried in the church chancel in 1637. (The chancel is the part of a church near the altar, usually separated by a rail.)

[101] Eleanor Sayer Holt, *The Second Church of Elizabeth City Parish, 1623/4–1698, An Historical-Archaeological Report* (Hampton, Va., 1985). The dimensions of the Elizabeth City church was 23 feet x 52 feet with an 8-foot x 9-foot entrance.

[102] Anne Floyd Upshur and Ralph T. Whitelaw, "Some New Thoughts concerning the Earliest Settlements on the Eastern Shore of Virginia." *The Virginia Magazine of History and Biography* 50, no. 3 (1942): 193-98. Accessed May 30, 2021. http://www.jstor.org/stable/4245176.

was anywhere but at the end of the peninsula where—in Upshur and Whitelaw's day—Fort Custis was located. (It's now the Eastern Shore of Virginia National Wildlife Refuge.) Regarding the name Old Plantation, they provided three theories.

The first theory—and the one they thought "most probable"—was that an overseer for the Dale Plantation had a settlement here; however, as discussed in Chapter 12, the Dale cattle and men weren't moved to the Eastern Shore until 1622. Upshur and Whitelaw, along with many others, made the mistake of thinking that Dales Gift had been the personal property of Dale. That old, "uncertain Rumor" led them astray, as rumors often do.

They characterized their second theory as "not so promising;" this theory was that "the name came from the early settlement of John Blower." Upshur and Whitelaw believed that John Blore's patent was issued in 1623, although they qualified that he could have lived there some time before.[103] Based on this assumption, they questioned whether Blore's patent "could have been early enough to be the answer to the problem."

Upshur and Whitelaw's third theory regarding Old Plantation was that Thomas Savage may have had a trading post on the neck that later came to be known as the "Old Plantation;" however, this theory was presented as a nod to Savage's early trading activity on the Shore. The authors concluded that Savage's residence on the Shore "could not have been quite so early as previously claimed, and that there seems to be no record to authenticate his actual date of settlement."

Of these three theories, the one suggesting that Old Plantation referenced Blore's settlement seems most credible; however, credibility isn't always satisfactory. The first documented use of the name was in 1627 when John Wilcocks asked the governor and council for a patent of 500 acres "uppon the old plantation creeke" next to Blore.[104] About six

---

[103] Upshur and Whitelaw noted that the "Blower patent" was recorded on page 3 of the patent book, a page that is missing. They cited notes from W. B. Wooldridge who, apparently, determined that the Blower patent was issued in 1623. According to Nugent (Nugent, *Vol. 1*, p. 2), the only surviving information for the patent in question was: "John Blow, 150 acs., page 3." This may or may not be John Blore (Blower), as his patent was always noted to be 140 acres, even up to 1645 when Peter Walker absorbed it into his own patent (see Nugent, *Vol. 1*, 159, 534).

[104] McIlwaine, *Minutes*, 146.

months later, the governor and council heard from an unnamed source that "divers planters at Accawmacke doe intend at the old plantation Creeke and at Magety-Bay on that shoare to erect some new plantations." They deliberated and decided not to permit such a plan, "but rather to keepe them, as much as may be, seated closely together."[105] Fourteen months later, the court granted Charles Harmar permission to take 100 acres "upon the southerly side of the old plantation Creeke." (This was when that "uncertaine Rumor" surfaced about Lady Dale's property.)[106] Harmar's allowance was the beginning of official expansion outside the original settlement bounds; however, the next allowance for land south of Old Plantation Creek would not be granted for six more years.

If we look just at the years between Blore and the 1624/25 muster, we can be certain that the Eastern Shore settlement was no larger than an area of five miles by two miles. In these nearly five years, the population increased from Blore's two or so people to fifty-one people. The number of dwellings increased from one to twenty. If each new household was considered a "new plantation," doesn't it stand to reason that Blore's was indeed the old plantation? Granted, it doesn't seem like enough time went by to warrant the adjective "old;" however, time is always relative within a context. If you bought a new suit this year, wouldn't the one you bought last year be your "old" suit?

Credible but not satisfactory.

Upshur and Whitelaw missed a fourth theory, and this is the one I find credible and satisfactory. This theory isn't new, but my idea of it is a bit different from that of others.

The most intriguing version of this next theory was proffered by Dr. Susie Ames. Dr. Ames theorized that Dale directed the establishment of a Company Garden on the neck now called Old Plantation and that it was called "Dale's Gift." The purpose of the garden would have been to produce commodities such as hemp and flax for the Company's profit. In May of 1617, when Argall returned to Virginia as the new Deputy Governor, a place called "the Companies Garden" was turned over to his management. It was said that this garden had "yeilded to them in one year about £300 profitt." Also turned over to his management were

---

[105] McIlwaine, *Minutes*, 156. Magety Bay at this time was on the bayside, in the area below Old Plantation Creek.
[106] McIlwaine, *Minutes*, 179.

"Servants: 54 imployed in the same Garden and in Saltworks sett upp for the service of the Collony."[107] Based on those four lines alone, it's easy to see how Dr. Ames came to her theory. The only drawback I see is that when Dale left in 1616, only seventeen men were employed at "Dales Gift," and according to Rolfe, those men were assigned to salt and fish. Rolfe accounted for all the farmers in the colony, and none were on the Eastern Shore.

My version of the fourth theory is that the men of the salt and fishing operation used this site—the lower end of today's Old Plantation Neck—to quarter during the winter and summer. Rolfe had said these men were fed and maintained by the Company, which probably meant that they didn't have to worry about planting corn, but even the soldiers at Point Comfort supplemented what the common store provided.[108]

Consider this: If the salt and fishing operation were seasonal (as Rolfe said), did the crew spend all four seasons at the same site? Neither winter nor summer is as agreeable on the sea coast as it is inside the bay. If no one was forcing them to stay, why wouldn't they go to a milder location for the off-season work of repairing salt pans and fishing gear? And why wouldn't they take the opportunity to put in and tend a crop? In such a scenario, Lieutenant Cradock's crew had a worksite for two seasons and a plantation site for the other two seasons.

If John Blore had indeed been a member of Lieutenant Cradock's salting and fishing crew, he would have thoroughly known the land that the crew used. When Governor Yeardley asked him to give up his land at Falling Creek, and perhaps suggested that Blore could plant anywhere else, Blore might have said something like, "I want the old plantation site on the eastern shore." (Such phrasing would distinguish it from the old saltworks site.)

In Chapter 13, I asked where the werowance might have placed the boundary for Dales Gift and suggested that Ackomack River (Cherrystone Inlet) would have been a good place. Designating such a boundary wouldn't have meant that the Indians vacated the land; the boundary would have been for the English. At the time, the English wished only to have a small presence on the Eastern Shore: a fish and salt operation, a small farm for corn and tobacco, perhaps a trading post, and

---

[107] Kingsbury, *VCR-1*, 350.
[108] Hamor, 33.

a lookout on the bay. Given that as a possibility, seven years later Yeardley would have found it unnecessary to ask the werowance's permission for Blore's activity. A message through Thomas Savage would have been sufficient. It wasn't until after the Indian attack that Yeardley would have found it necessary to conference with the werowance about a new, major plan for English settlement on the Eastern Shore.

Imagine the advantage Blore would have had if this theory is accurate. The land was cleared. Rough shelter had survived, good enough to repair and live in while making a proper dwelling. The boat landing was shaped and staked. Blore knew the channel and he knew the creek. Also, after three years of experience, he knew the habits of the nearby native people.

Credible and satisfactory.

The early records seldom say just "old plantation" or "old plantation creek." It was called "the old plantation" and "the old plantation creek." That language reflects dialogue. My guess is that it started with Blore himself as he reported to friends that the governor had given him the go-ahead to claim his patent at the old plantation. It has an affectionate ring to it. "Over at the old plantation, more than half the work's already done," he might've said. "Means more time to spend with the missus."

Across the creek from Blore's plantation is a point of land that was known as "the fishing point." The creek's channel almost touches the land here over a hole about nine feet deep (U. S. Coast & Geodetic Survey chart in 1872). Just below Blore's land was a nine-foot-deep trough that brought the channel to the edge of the land. I suggest that each of these features added to the site's attraction for habitation and commerce.

The fishing point had probably been a popular spot long before the English came, but once they were here, it served as a meeting place. Twenty years later, the point would host a victualing house (tavern) where the court held their meetings.

A maddening issue in the old plantation story is that an early writer said it was the site of the Eastern Shore's first church, and this remark led some other writers astray.[109] The actual sequence of events of the early Eastern Shore English occupation precludes the possibility that the first church was here. It's another fascinating story for another day.

---

[109] That writer is usually referred to as "an early chronicler," but neither the identity nor the work of that chronicler has ever been discovered.

Company Land or Wilcocks's Plantation?

When Pory placed his ten tenants on the Eastern Shore in the fall of 1621, he said the Secretary's Land was near Ackomack, and he parenthetically identified Ackomack as "Captaine Wilcocks plantation."[110] That incidental clarification (and Pory's further report of mustering the Company tenants before he left) is the core piece of documentation to all theories about the beginning of a permanent settlement. Nora Miller Turman, a local historian, succinctly stated the following: "In the fall of 1620 Governor Yeardley sent a group of men in [the] charge of Captain John Wilcox to the Eastern Shore and English people have been here ever since."[111] The conclusion seems correct, but certainly not the date; and also, Turman's premise omits the importance of Deputy Nuce to Wilcocks's presence on the Eastern Shore.

Wilcocks arrived in Virginia in October of 1620 on the same voyage as Nuce. To have been on the Eastern Shore in that same fall in charge of a group of men would mean that he probably knew Yeardley beforehand (that's possible), that a boat and supplies were ready (that's possible), and that the issues of seasoning didn't hamper the plan (one could season on the Eastern Shore as well or better than in Elizabeth City). It's possible, but is it probable?

For all intents and purposes, the difference between what Mrs. Turman wrote and what I have theorized about Wilcocks's presence at Ackomack is minor. No doubt exists that Captain John Wilcocks was on the Eastern Shore when Secretary John Pory placed ten men nearby in the late summer or early fall of 1621.

The question now is whether Wilcocks's Plantation, Ackomack, was private or public? Was this Company land? a patent? or something else?

We can rule out that it was a patent because no documentation of a patent exists for Wilcocks until 1627 when he asked for 500 acres next to Blore. The first patents for Ackomack neck date from 1626. Some of these early patents clearly state that the land had belonged to the late Company and was now appointed to the public. (The Company was dissolved in 1624.) The total acreage for these combined Ackomack

---

[110] Smith, *Generall Historie*, 274.
[111] Nora Miller Turman, *The Eastern Shore of Virginia 1603-1964* (Onancock, Va., Eastern Shore News, Inc., 1964), 6.

neck patents was 140 acres. Language in the patents identified twenty of those acres as having been "late in the service & occupation of Capt. John Wilcocks."[112] All of that land was part of and within a larger area known as the "precincts of the Plantation of Accomack." Repeating that: the Company land was a part of the Plantation of Accomack. What does that mean?

To answer that question, we look at the context of events. In September of 1622, Governor Wyatt commissioned Sir George Yeardley to take groups of men and soldiers "to make warr, kill, spoile, and take by force or otherwise whatsoever boote [booty] of corn." On the same day that the governor wrote Yeardley's new commission, John Wilcocks was in Elizabeth City, preparing to go to war.[113] Yeardley at this time was on the Eastern Shore under commission to prepare a place for 300 to 400 colonists. Conceivably, it was in the months of Yeardley's "Eastern Shore Commission" that the Plantation of Accomack was created and Company land was carved out within it. Within the new plantation area was Wilcocks's original "Ackomack plantation."

When attempting to frame events that happened so long ago, a tendency exists to jump from date to date. For example, it's known when Governor Wyatt told Yeardley to go to the Eastern Shore (June 20); when Governor Wyatt told Yeardley to go to war (September 10); and when Wilcocks wrote his will (September 10). However, events did not happen in a vacuum 400 years ago any more than they do today. I bring this up because of Wilcocks's will.

In his will, Wilcocks identified himself as "of Ackomack." He said he was "intending to transport himself for a piece of service against and upon the Indians," and he signed the will in Elizabeth City. Looking at the dates, we might think this had nothing to do with Wyatt's commission to Yeardley. How could Wilcocks, who wrote his will in Elizabeth City, know what the governor was doing that day in James City?

I suggest that Wilcocks knew Yeardley's war commission was in the works because Yeardley knew it. Yeardley had served as a right-hand man to the new governor, and this is likely to have continued through messengers. Wyatt wasn't making unilateral decisions. Just because

---

[112] Library of Virginia, "Virginia Land Grants and Patents" (https://lva-virginia.libguides.com/land-grants).
[113] Kingsbury, *VCR-3*, 678–679.

Yeardley was on the Eastern Shore didn't mean he didn't get and receive communications from Wyatt who was on the mainland.

Imagine that Wilcocks was the first person Yeardley met with while on the Eastern Shore. In discussions with the key players, it was decided that the best place for 300 to 400 people would be right where Wilcocks was seated. Yeardley likely offered Wilcocks the command of the new settlement, but when Yeardley told him that his next assignment would be a march against the Indians, Wilcocks (possibly a career soldier) opted to go to war. If not Wilcocks to command the new plantation, including Company land and tenants, then who?

According to his commission, Yeardley had the authority to choose a commander. William Epps happened to be present and available.

In the aftermath of the March 22nd Indian attack, William Epps and his brother Peter rescued four servants from another plantation.[114] The Epps, five of their servants, and the rescued four came to the Eastern Shore, possibly under the sails of Yeardley's Eastern Shore Commission. William Epps had a history with Yeardley.

In the early months of Yeardley's governorship, Epps was acting as commander at Smyths Hundred when he killed a man. The jury found Epps guilty of manslaughter "by chance meddley," and Governor Yeardley returned him to the command at Smyths. John Rolfe had noted that Yeardley thought Epps showed promise.

Yeardley chose Epps to command the new plantation called Ackomack. Company land was designated within this plantation, and preparation was made for the receipt of 300 to 400 colonists. (That grand plan would be severely pruned when word came from Sir Edwin Sandys, charging that it was treasonous to even think of such a thing.) When Wilcocks returned from the war march, he again took up residence in Ackomack, but only on a twenty-acre part where his dwelling stood. William Epps continued as the commander. That next January, Wilcocks was elected as a burgess to represent Ackomack along with Lady Dale's former overseer, Henry Watkins.

In summary, I believe Wilcocks's plantation, Ackomack, started out as a quasi-private plantation with help from leased Company tenants.

---

[114] McIlwaine, *Minutes*, 91, 138–139. Henry Wilson, Thomas Powell, Christopher Barker, and William Munns were among Captain John Ward's servants who were rescued.

Whatever it was and whatever Wilcocks had planned for it to be, the Indians' March 22nd attack shattered those plans and set into motion the formation of a new colony plantation including Company land, all commanded by Captain William Epps.

John Smith's Account of Yeardley's Visit to the Eastern Shore

Governor Wyatt's June 20, 1622, commission to Yeardley is extraordinary in that it called for Yeardley to find an apt place for up to 400 men. According to the commission, Yeardley was to leave enough men in this place to make the beginning of a plantation. The commission, in whole, reads [with superscripts spelled out]:

June 20, 1622

A Commission to Sir George Yeardley for the Easterne Shore &c

Whereas through the large extention of ground heretofore graunted, both to Comporations, Hundreds, particuler Plantations, and private Dividends, this Colony was so dispersed & people so straglingly seated, that we were not only bereft of the frendly comerce and mutuall societie one of another in religeous duties, the first fruits of Civility; but were also disabled any way to provide for the common safety either against forraine or domesticke invasion, the carefullest charge of Christian charity, wittnes those vexed Soules and troubled Spirits of ours, when in this last outrage of these Infidells we were forced to stand and gaze at our distressed brethren, fryinge in the furies of our enimies, and could not relieve them. And whereas throug these occasions, We have been forced to quitt most of our habitations, so that many of our people are not unsetled. These are therefore, both to provide for the good of the one, and prevent the danger of the other, (such places as we now hould in this River, being already filled with sufficient numbers) to desire, and require you Sir George Yeardley knight, and on[e] of his Majesties Counsell established for Virginia, to levy at your best conveniencie, such a number of the people of this Colony, as for this present intended imploy- ment shall by you be thought sufficient; and that imbarking your self and said Company, in such Shipps Pinaces or Shallops, as you shall make choise of, you presently depart out of this River in discovery both of the West and Eastern Shores of this Bay, or any other of our Sea Coasts, which shall seeme best unto you within the limits of 33 and 40 degrees of Northerly latitude, there to search for and find out some convenient place, both for quantity and quality of ground apt safely to entertaine some three or foure hundred men, uppon which, or uppon any other place whatsoever, that in your discrescion you shall think fitt for your present necessity and use, it shalbe lawfull for you presently to sett downe, and leave such and so many of our Colony as are now under your Command, to make a begining there for a Plantation, giving to every one of them foure acres of land for his particular employment, placing your present buildings in such forme as may be by addition of numbers intended to be sent imediatly after the Cropp, capable of fortification; for the better execution whereof. These are to give you full power and command over all our people that shall accompany you in this vioadge, or that you shall find inhabiting in any of those precincts aforesaid, and to punish them according to theire delinquencie, and the necessitie of the occasion. And because through the late revolt and failinge off, of our Neighbouringe Savages, we are uncertaine of frendshipp with any of those Natives, These are to give you leave, and absolute power, either to make peace or warr with any of them, as it shall seeme most behoofull and necessarie for the present estate of this our Common-Wealth, as also peaceably to trade for Furrs, Corne, or any other Comodities, with such as shalbe frends, and forceably to take such or the like from those that dare be our enemies. Itt is also thought expedient, and graunted to you Sir George Yeardley knight, that if in this your passage, you shalbe chased or encountred, by any man of Warr, or other Saile whatsoever, that shall go about to hinder these your proceedings, either by takeing away your provisions, or by offering any other such violence (except by his Majesties authoritie he be thereunto licensed0 that you may with all your power & uttmost endevors repell, resist, and defend your self, and our honors against that force, or anyother of like nature and condition, either outward or homeward bound, in all Harbors, or Rivers, members of the teritory of this Plantation. And to prohibitt, forbid, and compell there unto, any shipping of what

Nation soever within the said limits (without speciall Comission from his Majestie, or from his Majesties Counsell and Company of Virginia) from trade, fishing, or other bussines, then such as the law of Nature and Nations allow to every distressed person. And for your better ease in the execution of these imployments, John Pountis Vice-Admirall, and Counsellor of State here resident is requested freely to accompany you in this vioage, whose Counsell & advise you are desired to use in case of importance. given at James Citty under my hand & the great Seale of the Colony this 20th of June 1622. Francis Wyatt.[115]

Here's how John Smith characterized Yeardley's response to this commission:

About the latter end of June, Sir George Yearley accompanied with the Councell, and a number of the greatest Gallants in the Land, stayed three or foure daies with Captaine Nuse, he making his moane to a chiefe man amongst them for want of provision for his Company, the great Commander replied hee should turn them to his green Corne, which would make them plumpe and fat: these fields being so neere the Fort, were better regarded and preserved then the rest, but the great mans command, as we call them, was quickly obeied, for though it was scarce halfe growne either to the greatnesse or goodnesse, they devoured it greene though it did them small good. Sir George with his company went to Accomack to his new Plantation, where he staied neere six weekes; some Corne he brought home, but as he adventured for himselfe, he accordingly enjoyed the benefit [116]

Seven months later, the Virginia Council wrote to the Company in London, defending their actions since the attack. The Council addressed the Eastern Shore:

---

[115] Kingsbury, *VCR-3*, 656–657. [Some spelling was modernized] Using the calculation of 140 acres of land as noted above under the subheading "Company Land or Wilcocks's Plantation?" minus Wilcocks's twenty acres, the estimated number of men that Yeardley may have left at Ackomack is 30.
[116] Smith, *Generall Historie*, 302.

> *The Removeall to the Easterne shore which you calle an abandoninge of this River (beinge aplace indeede that Comands not only this but all the Rivers in the Baye, was a thinge only in dispute & speculations: But upon Consideratione, that it might be at first sight a taint to our reputa- tion, & noe way lawfull to forsake our stations withowt leave, it proceeded noe farther, as all our Actions since may Sufficyently prove* [117]

Two months after that, on March 28, 1623, George Sandys, the colony's treasurer, wrote from Virginia, saying that the idea of removing to the Eastern Shore was embarrassing. He and the governor had only discussed it, but they had never thought to go there, "though manie ranne violentlie that waye." [118]

Two days later, Sandys again talked of the situation in another letter. His exasperation with London's judgement seems apparent as he related that the Virginians were being characterized as indiscreet and cowardly for bringing colonists into safety. He noted that these colonists had neither food nor munitions; they couldn't defend themselves. They would have "perished either by the Enimye, or famyne." Sandys had heard from his brother, Sir Edwin, whose perception was that the colony, "strucke with a Panicke feare" had proposed to remove the colony to the Eastern Shore. George Sandys admitted that the governor and council had discussed removing to Eastern Shore, but he said they knew better than to do such a thing without the Company's permission. Still, he said, they did think it was a good idea to survey the place and to seat a party there. According to George Sandys, the Virginia leadership (including himself) had been accused of "treason against God and man." It was being suggested that they deserved to be hanged. [119]

It seems that John Smith never heard the "real" story, yet his is the tale we most often hear. In his version, Yeardley went to Elizabeth City and gave lame advice to Deputy Nuce (advice that was not unlike, "Let them eat cake."). Then he went to Ackomack, stayed six weeks, got some corn, and kept it for himself rather than sharing it with the starving colony. To know the reason John Smith so disparaged George Yeardley would be an interesting subject to explore; however, the only piece of

---

[117] Kingsbury, *VCR-4*, 11–12.
[118] Kingsbury, *VCR-4*, 67.
[119] Kingsbury, *VCR-4*, 73–74.

John Smith's account that I wish to deal with is his statement about Yeardley going "to Accomack to his new plantation."

Even though it stands to reason that John Smith was never privy to the correspondence between the Sandys brothers and therefore would never have known the secrecy that followed Yeardley's return from the Eastern Shore, Smith likely heard something. That Yeardley went by to see Captain Nuce is likely. That something happened regarding green corn is likely. That he visited his plantation on the Eastern Shore is likely. The question is: does this mean Yeardley received the plantation before this commission or does it mean he received it during this commission? If Smith were a solid source, we could accept this as an indication that the werowance had already given Yeardley permission for his land on the Eastern Shore. However, Smith is not a solid source. The timing of Yeardley's meeting with the werowance is still a matter of conjecture.

WY 8
HOME OF THE FIRST SETTLER

Thomas Savage, a lad of thirteen, arrived at Jamestown on 2 Jan. 1608 with Capt. Christopher Newport on the ship *John and Francis*. John Smith later wrote, "The next day Newport came a shore....A boy named Thomas Savage (whom Newport called son) was then given unto Powhatan." Savage resided several years with the Indians, growing up in association with Pocahontas. He became proficient in the Indian languages and later served as an interpreter. Savage settled on the Eastern Shore by 1619. There Debedeavon, the "Laughing King," gave him a large tract of land, perhaps 9,000 acres for increasing trade with the Indians.

DEPARTMENT OF HISTORIC RESOURCES, 1998

Final Thoughts

At the beginning of this project, I had in mind that Captain John Wilcocks was the first permanent colonist to the Eastern Shore. The sole "eye witness," Secretary John Pory, told us that Wilcocks was already here when he (Pory) placed the Secretary's tenants on the Secretary's land. This wasn't new information to me; Pory's words have been repeated dozens of times in books and articles. Nevertheless, the story most often told—indeed, the one that's published on the official highway marker—identifies Thomas Savage as the first settler. Just when I was about to write that Wilcocks is the name that should be on that marker, John and Frances Blore's story assembled itself with extraordinary clarity.

In no way do I wish to disparage Thomas Savage; he deserves a highway marker for being much more than "a first." However, the Blores' story stands, and it is as remarkable as any in those marvelous old records.

References

Ames, Susie M. *The Virginia Eastern Shore in the 17th Century* (New York, Russell & Russell, 1973 [original copyright 1940].

Brown, Alexander. *The First Republic in America* (Boston & New York: Houghton, Mifflin & Co.,1898). (hereafter: Brown, *First Republic*).

Chamberlain, John, 1554?-1628, and Norman Egbert McClure. *The Letters of John Chamberlain*. Philadelphia: The American philosophical society, 1939.

Connor, Seymour V. "Sir Samuel Argall: A Biographical Sketch." *The Virginia Magazine of History and Biography* 59, no. 2 (1951).

de Bry, Johann Theodore. "Samuel Argall - Chickahominy." Virginia Historical Society, 1618.

Dorman, John Frederick. *Adventures of Purse and Person, Virginia, 1607-1624/5: Families A-F*, (Baltimore: Genealogical Publishing Company, 2004).

Great Britain, William Noel Sainsbury et al., *Calendar of State Papers, Colonial Series, 1574–1660* (London: 1860).

Hamor, Ralph. *A True Discourse of the Present State of Virginia (Richmond, 1957* [orig. publ. London, 1615].

Holt, Eleanor Sayer. *The Second Church of Elizabeth City Parish, 1623/4–1698, An Historical-Archaeological Report* (Hampton, Va., 1985).

Kingsbury, Susan Myra, editor. *The Records of The Virginia Company of London. Vol. I-IV* (Washington, D.C.:Government Printing Office, 1906-1933).

"Kings Creek, 1952." NETRonline: Historic Aerials, n.d. http://www.historicaerials.com/.

Library of Virginia, "Virginia Land Grants and Patents (https://lva-virginia.libguides.com/land-grants).

Mackey, Howard and Marlene A. Groves, *Northampton County, Virginia, Record Book: Court Cases, Vol. 9, 1664–1674* (Rockport, ME: Picton Press, 2003).

Mariner, Kirk. *True Tales of the Eastern Shore* (Onancock, Va.: Miona Press, 2003).

McCartney, Martha W. *Virginia Immigrants and Adventurers: A Biographical Dictionary, 1607-1635* (Baltimore: Genealogical Publishing Co., 2007).

McIlwaine, H. R., editor. *Minutes of the Counsel and General Court, 1622–1630, 1670–1676* (Richmond: Virginia State Library, 1924).

Nehgs. The New England Historical and Genealogical Register, Volume 47, 1893 (Heritage Books, 2016).

Neill, Edward D. *History of the Virginia Company of London* (Albany, N.Y.: J. Munsell, 1869).

Northampton County, Virginia, Court Record Book No.1, 1632–1640.

Northampton County, Virginia, Court Record Book No. 2, 1640–1645.

Nugent, Nell Marion. Virginia Genealogical Society, and Virginia State Library, *Cavaliers And Pioneers: Abstracts of Virginia Land Patents And Grants, 1623-1800, Vol. 1* (Richmond: Press of the Dietz Print Co., 1934).

Perry, James R. *The Formation of a Society on Virginia's Eastern Shore 1615–1655* (Chapel Hill: University of North Carolina Press, 1990).

Purchas, Samuel. *Purchas His Pilgrimes: In Five Bookes, Vol. 4* (United Kingdom: n.p., 1625).

Ransome, David R. "Wives for Virginia, 1621." *The William and Mary Quarterly* 48, no. 1 (1991): 3-18. Accessed April 15, 2021. doi:10.2307/2937995.

Rolf[e], John. "A True Relation of the State of Virginia left by Sir Thomas Dale Knight in May last 1616." https://encyclopediavirginia.org/entries/a-true-relation-of-the-state-of-virginia-lefte-by-sir-thomas-dale-knight-in-may-last-1616-1617.

Smith, John. *The Generall Historie of Virginia, New England, & The Summer Isles* (London, 1624, Reprint, Bedford, Ma., Applewood Books, 2006).

Turman, Nora Miller. *The Eastern Shore of Virginia 1603-1964* (Onancock, Va., Eastern Shore News, Inc., 1964.

Upshur, Anne Floyd and Ralph T. Whitelaw, "Some New Thoughts concerning the Earliest Settlements on the Eastern Shore of Virginia." *The Virginia Magazine of History and Biography* 50, no. 3 (1942): 193-98. Accessed May 30, 2021. http://www.jstor.org/stable/4245176.

US Coast & Geodetic Survey. "CHESAPEAKE BAY. YORK RIVER HAMPTON ROADS CHESAPEAKE ENTRANCE. SHEET NO.1." 1863. Map. NOAA's Historical Map & Chart Collection. https://www.historicalcharts.noaa.gov/image.php?filename=LC00131_00_1863.

Van Zandt, Cynthia J. *Brothers Among Nations: Pursuit of Intercultural Alliances in Early America, 1560-1660* (Oxford University Press, 2008).

Wise, Jennings Cropper. *Ye Kingdome of Accawmacke, Or, The Eastern shore of Virginia in the Seventeenth Century* (Richmond: Bell Book, 1911).

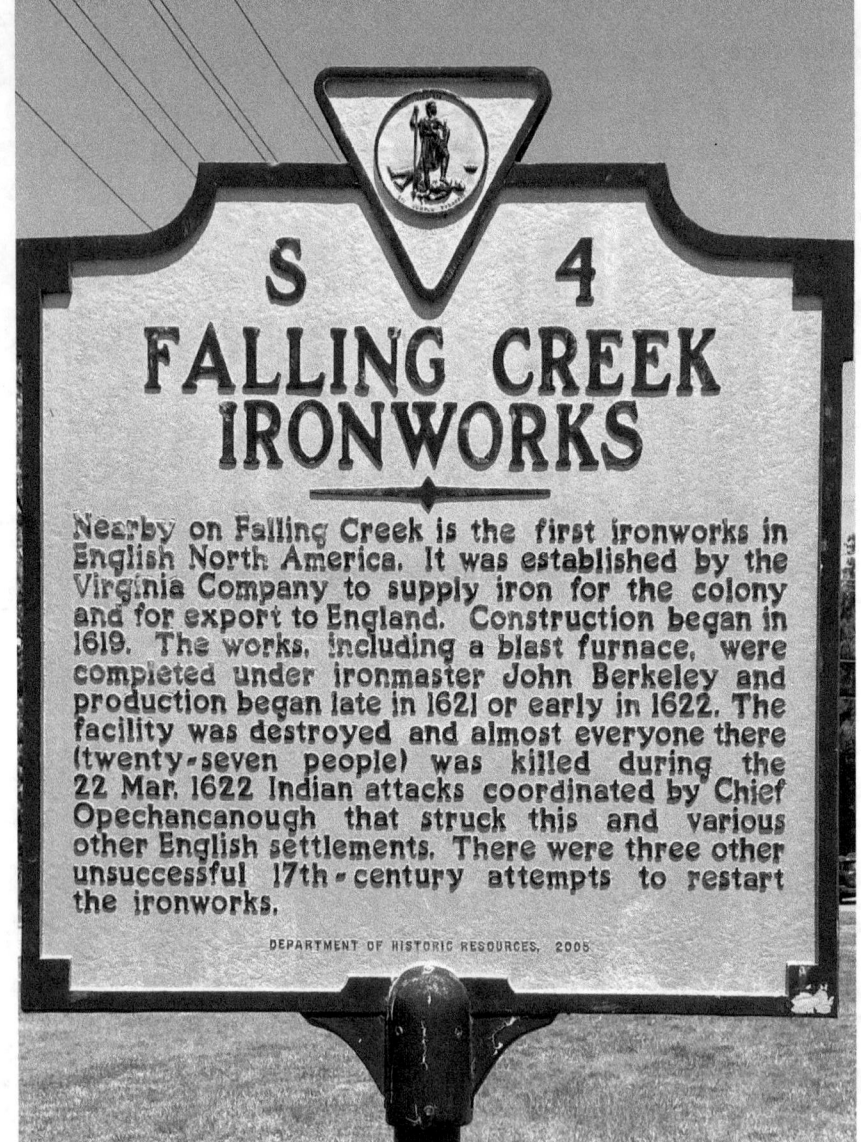

Index

Africans, Eastern Shore
    Alexander 40
    Anthony 40
    Cassanga 40
    Jane 40
    John 40
    Palatia 40
    Polonia 40
    Sebastian 40
Ames, Susie (Dr. Ames) 45, 61, 67, 68
Argall, Samuel 3, 4, 5, 7, 8, 10, 13, 14, 15, 37, 44, 45, 55, 56, 67
Argalls Guiffe (Gift) 19
Ball, Robert 64
Barker, Christopher 72
Barrow, Richard 9
Beheathland, Robert 14
Bermuda Hundred 5, 6, 8, 60
Berkeley, John 44
Berry, John 37
Blore, Frances *xvi, xvii,* 43, 47, 50, 63, 79
Blore, John *xvi, xvii,* 41, 43, 44, 45, 46, 47, 50, 51, 55, 61, 63, 64, 65, 66, 67, 68, 69, 70, 79
Bohun, Lawrence 14
Bolton, Francis 29
Brewer, Thomas 37

Buckroe 36
Bush, John 37
Cape Charles 2, 3, 5, 6, 56
Cape Henry 2, 3
Capps, William 37
Captain Lawnes Plantation 19
Captain Wards Plantation 19
Carleton, Dudley (1st Viscount Dorchester) 17
Charles City 9, 19, 29, 35
Colfer, (unknown) 57
commodities 23, 31, 32, 43, 67
Cradock, William 6, 45, 68
Craddock Creek 6
Dale, Elizabeth (known as Lady Dale) *xvii*, 56, 57, 58, 67, 72
Dale, Thomas 4, 5, 6, 7, 8, 9, 10, 26, 55, 56, 57, 58, 59, 60, 66, 67, 68
Dales Gift *xviii*, 4, 5, 6, 55, 58, 65, 66, 67, 68
Danvers, John 14
De La Warr, Lord (see West, Thomas) 8, 10, 13, 14, 15, 17
Dixon, Adam 37
East India Company 8
Elizabeth City *xvi*, 29, 30, 31, 33, 36, 37, 38, 44, 45, 46, 47, 49, 50, 51, 61, 64, 65, 70, 71, 76
Epps, William *xvii*, 19, 64, 72, 73
Falling Creek *xvi*, 44, 46, 51, 61, 68
fishing 4, 6, 19, 23, 24, 55, 68, 69
Flowerdew, Temperance (see Yeardley, Temperance) 9
Flowerdieu Hundred 19
Fort Monroe 36
Fox Hill 36
Gates, Thomas 7, 14, 15
General Assembly 18, 19, 37, 39, 44, 64
Gibbs, John 19
Gilbert, Bartholomew 2, 3
Gingaskin 64
Great Charter 8, 9, 10, 29, 35, 36, 44
Gundry, John 37, 44
Hamby, William 57

Hamor, Ralph 4, 7, 68
Hampton University 30, 36
Hampton VA Hospital 36
Harmar, Charles 56, 57, 67
Hawes, Nicholas 4
Henrico, Henricus 5, 9, 19, 20, 29, 35, 44, 45
Howe, John 64, 65
Indian werowance *xvii*, 3, 59, 60, 61, 62, 63, 64, 68, 69, 77
iron *xvi*, 23, 26, 27, 31, 32, 43, 44, 45
James I, (King) 8, 11
James City (Jamestown) *xv, xviii*, 3, 7, 9, 10, 13, 18, 19, 25, 29, 35, 46, 47, 50, 53, 56, 57, 71
Johnson, Robert 14
Julian, William 37
Kempe, William 37
Kicotan, Kecoughtan, Kiccowtan *xviii*, 5, 9, 19, 29, 30, 35, 36, 37, 45
Lake (Lacke), Frances (see Blore) 43, 46
Laughing King, Laughing Kings *xvii*, 53, 60, 64
Mainwaring, Philip (fn) 11
Martin Brandon 19
Martin, John 9, 37, 56, 60, 61
Martins Hundred 19
Mattawomes 62
Maydes (Maid) Town 41
Moll, Estinien 52
Munns, William 72
Nuce, Anne 51
Nuce, Thomas 20, 29, 30, 31, 32, 33, 36, 37, 38, 47, 49, 50, 51, 61, 64, 70, 76, 77
Nugent, Nell (fn) 19, 40, 58, 61, 66
Pocahontas (see Rolfe, Rebecca) 5
Pory, John *xvi*, 6, 17, 18, 19, 25, 26, 43, 44, 46, 51, 52, 53, 56, 59, 60, 61, 63, 70, 79
Powell, John 37
Powell, Thomas 72
Powhatan 3, 64
Prickett, Miles 44, 45, 46
Rolfe, John 5, 6, 40, 68, 72
Rolfe, Rebecca (Pocahontas) 5

salt 3, 4, 6, 23, 24, 26, 32, 44, 45, 46, 52, 55, 59, 68
Sandys, Edwin 11, 13, 17, 19, 21, 25, 26, 30, 31, 32, 40, 43, 44, 72, 76, 77
Sandys, George 53, 76, 77
Savage, Thomas xv, xvii, 53, 55, 56, 60, 61, 62, 63, 64, 66, 69, 79
Ships
    Bona Nova 29, 49
    Duty 25
    Falcon 9
    London Marchant 43
    Phoenix 3
    Sea Venture 7
Smith, John *xviii*, 3, 15, 52, 53, 59, 60, 61, 70, 73, 75, 76, 77
Smith (Smyth), Roger 14
Smith (Smyth), Thomas 11, 13, 19
Swift, James 14
Thorpe, George 20, 29, 44
Tucker, Daniel 14
Tucker, William 37
Turman, Nora Miller 70
Upshur, Anne Floyd *xviii, xix,* 65, 66, 67
Verrazzano, Giovanni da (fn) 2
Villiers, George (Marquis of Buckingham) 31
Ward, John 19, 72
Watkins, Henry (fn) 57, 72
Watkins, Perregrim 64
West, Francis 14, 15
West, Thomas (3rd Baron DeLaWarr) 8
Whitelaw, Ralph T. *xviii, xix,* 65, 66, 67
Willoby, Thomas 37
Wilson, Henry 72
Wolstenholm, John 14
Wyatt, Francis *xvii,* 53, 62, 71, 72, 73, 75
Wilcocks, John *xvi, xvii, xviii,* 20, 47, 49, 50, 51, 52, 53, 55, 61, 63, 64, 66, 70, 71, 72, 73, 75, 79
Wriothesley, Thomas (Earl of Southampton) 19
Yeardley, Argoll (fn) 14
Yeardley, George *xv, xvi, xvii,* 7, 8, 9, 10, 11, 13, 14, 15, 17, 18, 19, 20, 25, 30, 31,

36, 37, 38, 39, 40, 44, 45, 46, 49, 50, 51, 52, 53, 56, 57, 60, 61, 62, 68, 69, 70, 71, 72, 73, 74, 75, 76, 77

Yeardley, Temperance 9, 14

Yeardley, Elizabeth (fn) 10

A FEW NOTES BEFORE YOU BEGIN

1. In these early years, England still used the Julian or old style (o.s.) calendar in which the legal year began on March 25. In this book, double years are used for dates between January 1 and March 24; the first year is old style and the second year is new style (n.s.) as in 1632/33 (o.s./n.s.).

1. ENGLISH BOOTS AND BOATS

1. Cynthia J. Van Zandt, *Brothers Among Nations: Pursuit of Intercultural Alliances in Early America, 1560-1660* (Oxford University Press, 2008), 50–51. While Gilbert's exploration may have been the first documented English landing, other explorers' writings have suggested earlier landings. For an excellent description of Giovanni da Verrazzano's possible landing on Virginia's Eastern Shore, see Jennings Cropper Wise, *Ye Kingdome of Accawmacke, Or, The Eastern shore of Virginia in the Seventeenth Century* (Richmond: Bell Book, 1911), 6–9.
2. Northampton's county seal includes 1603, commemorating the county as the first place Englishmen stepped ashore in Virginia. The seal also includes 1620 (the year of the first permanent English settlement) and 1634 (the year the county was created by the colonial Grand Assembly).
3. The group was accompanied by the *Phoenix* at Cape Henry from where Smith and his crew left to begin their exploration in the barge. They returned to the James River in the barge. John Smith, *The Generall Historie of Virginia, New England, & The Summer Isles* (London, 1624, Reprint, Bedford, Ma., Applewood Books, 2006), 115, 123 (hereafter: Smith, *Generall Historie*).
4. Smith, *Generall Historie,* 115–116. In his account of this 1608 meeting, Smith did not name the Indian werowance. The story of Smith's encounter with the Eastern Shore Indians can also be found in: Kirk Mariner, *True Tales of the Eastern Shore* (Onancock, Va.: Miona Press, 2003), 14–16. *Salvage* was an early spelling of "savage;" a term the early English often used, categorizing the native people as primitive and uncivilized.
5. Purchas, Samuel. *Purchas His Pilgrimes: In Five Bookes* (United Kingdom: n.p., 1625), Vol. 4, 1765. Argall wrote this in a letter to Nicholas Hawes, June 1613.
6. Ralph Hamor, A True Discourse of the Present State of Virginia (Richmond, 1957 [orig. publ. London, 1615]), 21.

2. JOHN ROLFE'S REPORT

1. *Kequoughtan, Kiccowtan, Kicotan*, etc. In these early years, the spelling varied with each writer. This was the same for the name Henrico which was also spelled as *Henricus*.
2. John Rolf[e], "A True Relation of the State of Virginia left by Sir Thomas Dale Knight

in May last 1616." https://encyclopediavirginia.org/entries/a-true-relation-of-the-state-of-virginia-lefte-by-sir-thomas-dale-knight-in-may-last-1616-1617/

3. Perry, James R. *The Formation of a Society on Virginia's Eastern Shore, 1615-1655* (Chapel Hill: The University of North Carolina Press, 2012), 15. The word "sea" was used in reference to both the ocean and the bay, so it is of no help in determining the location of Cradock's camp. Pory's description of Smith Island and the mainland of Cape Charles is found in Susan Myra Kingsbury, ed. *The Records of The Virginia Company of London. Vol. I-IV* (Washington, D.C.:Government Printing Office, 1906-1933), 304 (hereafter: Kingsbury, *VCL-1, VCL-2, VCL-3* or *VCL-4*).
4. Kingsbury, *VCL-3*, 91. The idea that fishing had moved to the Potomack
5. The Eastern Shore of Virginia National Wildlife Refuge (http://www.fws.gov/refuge/eastern_shore_of_virginia/).

3. CAPTAIN GEORGE YEARDLEY

1. Kingsbury, *VCR-3*, 217. Great Britain, William Noel Sainsbury et al., *Calendar of State Papers, Colonial Series, 1574–1660* (London: 1860), 20 (hereafter: Sainsbury, Calendar).
2. Kingsbury, *VCR-3*, 98–109.
3. The James City 1624/25 muster shows that Elizabeth was 6 years old when that muster was taken, and that she had been born in Virginia. It is, of course, possible that she was born in 1618.
4. Chamberlain, John, 1554?-1628, and Norman Egbert McClure. *The Letters of John Chamberlain*. Philadelphia: The American philosophical society, 1939, 188.
5. Yeardley was designated by his military rank in his 1618 commission ("the Great Charter").
6. Kingsbury, *VCR-3*, 216–218.
7. Alexander Brown, *The First Republic in America* (Cambridge: Riverside Press, 1898), 293–294. The courtier was Philip Mainwaring.

4. IN THE WAKE OF CAPTAIN ARGALL

1. Connor, Seymour V. "Sir Samuel Argall: A Biographical Sketch." *The Virginia Magazine of History and Biography* 59, no. 2 (1951): 173. Accessed March 23, 2021. http://www.jstor.org/stable/4245766.
2. Kingsbury, *VCR-2*, 55.
3. Kingsbury, *VCR-3*, 417. Argall Yeardley's birth is determined from the 1624/25 muster. He was four years old in January 1624/25; therefore, his birth would have been in 1620 or 1621. A spelling often used for the son's name is "Argoll."
4. Kingsbury, *VCR-2*, 27.
5. Kingsbury, *VCR-3*, 119.
6. Kingsbury, *VCR-3*, 231. John Smith cast Yeardley in an unfavorable light, and portrayed Argall as nearly heroic. According to Smith, Yeardley was ineffective as a leader and prone to look after his own interests (see Smith, *Generall Historie*, 240, 302). However, the records of the Virginia Company reveal failings in the character of each man, but neither emerges as a villain nor a hero. Smith was not a primary player in the colony after he left in 1609 and probably took his cues in this instance from factions that disfavored Yeardley.

5. SECRETARY JOHN PORY

1. Brown, *The First Republic*, 294. This letter was to Dudley Carleton, 1st Viscount Dorchester.
2. Kingsbury, *VCR-3*, 222.
3. Kingsbury, *VCR-3*, 126.
4. Kingsbury, *VCR-3*, 251, 222.
5. Kingsbury, *VCR-3*, 251. Pory no doubt was referencing Matthew 5:18 and meant to spell "tittle." A tittle is an old word for the superscript dot over the letter i. The phrase "iota and tittle" indicates attention to the smallest detail.
6. Kingsbury, *VCR-3*, 153–179.
7. Jamestown Rediscovery, "The First General Assembly," historic-jamestowne.org.
8. An error in the introduction of Nell Nugent's first volume of Virginia land-patent abstracts may have led some researchers astray on this matter. Nugent reported that the first General Assembly had two Eastern Shore representatives, Captain Ward and Lieutenant Gibbs; however, this statement is inaccurate. Nell Marion Nugent, Virginia Genealogical Society, and Virginia State Library, *Cavaliers And Pioneers: Abstracts of Virginia Land Patents And Grants, 1623–1800, Vol. 1* (Richmond: Press of the Dietz Print Co., 1934), xxi, (hereafter: Nugent, Vol. 1). Captain John Ward's plantation was on the James River. Nugent may have made the assumption that Ward was from the Eastern Shore based on where his remaining servants were in 1622, after William Epps rescued them and took them to the Eastern Shore. (Scant evidence suggests that Ward may have been among the fishermen assigned to the Eastern Shore, but at the time of the Assembly, that fishing operation was defunct.)
9. Kingsbury, *VCR-3*, 216–217.
10. Kingsbury, *VCR-1*, 349, 382.

6. THE BROADSIDE

1. Kingsbury, *VCR-3*, 275–280.

7. PORY'S OPINION

1. Kingsbury, *VCR-3*, 300–306.

8. DEPUTY THOMAS NUCE

1. Kingsbury, *VCR-3*, 375, 406.
2. Kingsbury, *VCR-1*, 340.
3. Kingsbury, *VCR-3*, 485. The Virginia Company was using the new name by May 17, 1620; see Kingsbury, *VCR-1*, 349.
4. Kingsbury, *VCR-1*, 340.
5. Kingsbury, *VCR-3*, 297.
6. Kingsbury, *VCR-3*, 295. George Villiers was the Marquis of Buckingham at that time.
7. Kingsbury, *VCR-3*, 455–456.
8. Kingsbury, *VCR-3*, 647; *VCR-4*, 185. "Pensions" in this case would have been as an allowance or a guaranteed salary.
9. Kingsbury, *VCR-4*, 232.

9. "THE BURROUGH OF KICCOWTAN"

1. Kingsbury, *VCR-3*, 590.
2. While the Charter referred to the four areas as boroughs, the use of this administrative term did not survive. Kiccowtan was also spelled as Kiquotan, Kecoughtan, and Kicotan. Kicotan is one of the oldest spellings, and therefore, the one used most often in this account.
3. Kingsbury, *VCR-3*, 227. (Incidentally, this is adequate documentation that the name "Newport News" had nothing to do with the Nuce family, a theory that is still bandied about on occasion.)
4. Kingsbury, *VCR-3*, 123
5. Kingsbury, *VCR-1*, 460–461.
6. Martha W. McCartney, *Virginia Immigrants and Adventurers: A Biographical Dictionary, 1607-1635* (Baltimore: Genealogical Publishing Co., 2007), 440. Kingsbury, *VCR-2*, 44–45. Probably because of the colony's governmental collapse caused by the 1622 Indian attack, the cases weren't heard again until 1624. By that time, it seems everyone had an opinion about what to do for the displaced planters of Kicotan. Captain John Martin was advising them not to pay taxes until restitution was made to them. On January 3, 1624/25, Governor Wyatt and the council heard from William Julian, Sargeant Williams, and John Powell. Each of these men was given restitution in the form of tobacco, "wherewith he is well contented and satisfied which is the Company's desire" (H. R. McIlwaine, ed., *Minutes of the Counsel and General Court, 1622- 1630, 1670-1676* (Richmond: Virginia State Library, 1924), 41 (hereafter: McIlwaine, *Minutes*).

10. ALSO HAPPENING IN THE COLONY

1. Kingsbury, *VCR-3*, 243. Recent scholars have identified the ship as an English privateer, not a Dutch man-of-war.
2. This theory is based on the 1623/24 muster that showed thirteen Negro servants in Yeardley's count and nine other Negro servants in five other places of the colony.
3. Nugent, *Vol. 1*, 28. Northampton County, Court Book, No. 1, 52.
4. Ransome, David R. "Wives for Virginia, 1621." *The William and Mary Quarterly* 48, no. 1 (1991): 3-18. Accessed April 15, 2021. doi:10.2307/2937995.
5. Kingsbury, *VCR-2*, 26. When the Company gave approval for Maids Town, they had not yet heard about the March 22, 1621/22 attack in Virginia. The plan for Maids Town was never realized.

11. JOHN AND FRANCES BLORE

1. Kingsbury, *VCR-3*, 300–301; Vol. 1, 351. Frances's maiden name is taken from her will in which she named her siblings. Her will spelled the name as Lake and as Lacke (see Northampton County, *Court Book* No. 2, 61). A *tun* is a large cask capable of holding 252 gallons of liquid. A 300-tun ship would theoretically hold 300 such casks.
2. Kingsbury, *VCR-3*, 305.
3. Kingsbury, *VCR-3*, 710–711.
4. Kingsbury, *VCR-3*, 464, 475–476, 640.
5. Kingsbury, *VCR-3*, 507.

6. Dr. Ames was also of the opinion that John Blower had been one of Lieutenant Cradock's seventeen men at Smith Island, and that he was "one of the earliest permanent settlers on the Eastern Shore" (Susie M. Ames, *The Virginia Eastern Shore in the 17th Century* (New York, Russell & Russell, 1973 [original copyright 1940]), 21).
7. Kingsbury, *VCR-4*, 552, 559. Blore's name was spelled as Blower in this early record. I have used Blore, a later spelling from the Northampton County court records; however, it should be noted that Blower was a commonly used spelling of the name.
8. Kingsbury, *VCR-3*, 494.
9. John Camden Hotten, ed., The Original Lists of Persons of Quality: Emigrants, Religious, Exiles, Political Rebels, Serving Men Sold for a Term of Years, Apprentices, Children Stolen, Maidens Pressed, And Others, Who Went From Great Britain to the American Plantations, 1600–1700 (London: Empire State Book Co, 1874), 188–189. Jennifer Potter, The Jamestown Brides (London: Atlantic Books, 2018), 261–263.

12. JOHN WILCOCKS

1. Martha W. McCartney, *Virginia Immigrants and Adventurers: A Biographical Dictionary, 1607-1635* (Baltimore: Genealogical Publishing Co., 2007), 745.
   John Frederick Dorman, *Adventures of Purse and Person, Virginia, 1607-1624/5: Families A-F,* (Baltimore: Genealogical Publishing Company, 2004), 69.
2. Kingsbury, Vol. 3, 406. While it is known that Wilcocks came on the *Bona Nova* in 1620, it is possible that he came earlier in the year; however, only this one voyage of the *Bona Nova* in 1620 was found in the records.
3. nationalarchives.gov.uk
4. McCartney, *Virginia Immigrants*, 519.
5. Kingsbury, *VCR-3*, 458.
6. Kingsbury, *VCR-3*, 585.
7. McIlwaine, *Minutes*, 148.
8. John Smith, *Generall Historie*, 274. By saying that ten men were "meanly" provided, Pory tells us that he was not sent the twenty men that were promised. In this sense, "meanly" implies a meaning such as "cheaply."
9. Kingsbury, *VCR-4*, 107. This observation was made by George Sandys in a letter to John Ferrar, dated April 8, 1623.
10. John Smith, *Generall Historie*, 276.
11. Kingsbury, *VCR-3*, 471.
12. Kingsbury, *VCR-3*, 475, 479.
13. Kingsbury, *VCR-3*, 479, 488.

13. THOMAS SAVAGE, DALES GIFT, AND LADY DALE'S PEOPLE

1. Alexander Brown, *The First Republic in America* (Boston & New York: Houghton, Mifflin & Co.,1898), 420.
   Edward D. Neill, *History of the Virginia Company of London* (Albany, N.Y.: J. Munsell, 1869), 111. Most likely, trade with the Indians had been taking place since Savage first visited the Shore with Captain Argall in 1614, but Martin and Savage did not formalize the trade relationship until after 1619 under Governor Yeardley's direction.

2. Kingsbury, *Vol. 3*, 303.
3. McIlwaine, *Minutes*, 179. Harmar had been an overseer of Lady Dale's cattlemen.
4. Nehgs. The New England Historical and Genealogical Register, Volume 47, 1893. N.p.: Heritage Books, 2016, 403.
5. McIlwaine, *Minutes*, 192.
6. McIlwaine, *Minutes*, 48. The succession of Lady Dale's overseers in this first decade appears to have been Colfer, Henry Watkins, Charles Harmar, and William Hamby.
7. Kingsbury, *Vol. 1*, 491–492.
8. Kingsbury, *Vol. 4*, 12.
9. From England on May 20, 1622, Lady Dale complained that "her people in Virginia doe not performe covenants with her according to their Contracts" (Kingsbury, *Vol. 2*, 14). When this was written, another month would pass before word of the attack reached England.
10. Kingsbury, *Vol. 3*, 643.
11. Northampton County, Va., *Court Book No. 2*, 36.
12. Nugent, *Vol. 1*, 163.

14. THOMAS SAVAGE AND GEORGE YEARDLEY

1. Smith, *Generall Historie*, 276.
2. Smith, *Generall Historie*, 277.
3. Kingsbury, *Vol. 4*, 514
4. Dorman, *Adventures of Purse and Person*, 69
5. Nugent, Vol. 1, 30, 75. Howard Mackey and Marlene A. Groves, *Northampton County, Virginia, Record Book: Court Cases, Vol. 9, 1664–1674* (Rockport, ME: Picton Press, 2003), 152–153.
6. Smith, *Generall Historie*, 276. Dr. Ames also noted that Thomas Savage's land at Savage's Neck was probably allowed to him as a reward for his service (see Susie M. Ames, *The Virginia Eastern Shore in the 17th Century* (New York, Russell & Russell, 1973 [original copyright 1940]), 20).
7. The early records show that planters were required to purchase land from the native people before claiming it as their own. The negotiation was usually between the planter and the werowance. After clearing the ownership through the native people, the planter then acquired the English government's sanction for the land. That Savage's land was later called his "dividend" means that it was recognized as his rightful land based on service and/or headrights. (Personal investment [adventure] stock was also recognized for land grants, but no record shows that Savage owned Company stock.)
8. Kingsbury, *Vol. 3*, 656–657.

15. A FEW LOOSE THREADS

1. Northampton County, Va., *Court Book No. 1, 1632–1640*, 129. Commander John Howe was buried in the church chancel in 1637. (The chancel is the part of a church near the altar, usually separated by a rail.)
2. Eleanor Sayer Holt, *The Second Church of Elizabeth City Parish, 1623/4–1698, An Historical-Archaeological Report* (Hampton, Va., 1985). The dimensions of the Elizabeth City church was 23 feet x 52 feet with an 8-foot x 9-foot entrance.
3. Anne Floyd Upshur and Ralph T. Whitelaw, "Some New Thoughts concerning the

Earliest Settlements on the Eastern Shore of Virginia." *The Virginia Magazine of History and Biography* 50, no. 3 (1942): 193-98. Accessed May 30, 2021. http://www.jstor.org/stable/4245176.

4. Upshur and Whitelaw noted that the "Blower patent" was recorded on page 3 of the patent book, a page that is missing. They cited notes from W. B. Wooldridge who, apparently, determined that the Blower patent was issued in 1623. According to Nugent (Nugent, *Vol. 1*, p. 2), the only surviving information for the patent in question was: "John Blow, 150 acs., page 3." This may or may not be John Blore (Blower), as his patent was always noted to be 140 acres, even up to 1645 when Peter Walker absorbed it into his own patent (see Nugent, *Vol. 1*, 159, 534).
5. McIlwaine, *Minutes*, 146.
6. McIlwaine, *Minutes*, 156. Magety Bay at this time was on the bayside, in the area below Old Plantation Creek.
7. McIlwaine, *Minutes*, 179.
8. Kingsbury, *Vol. 1*, 350.
9. Hamor, 33.
10. That writer is usually referred to as "an early chronicler," but neither the identity nor the work of that chronicler has ever been discovered.
11. Smith, *Generall Historie*, 274.
12. Nora Miller Turman, *The Eastern Shore of Virginia 1603-1964* (Onancock, Va., Eastern Shore News, Inc., 1964), 6.
13. Library of Virginia, "Virginia Land Grants and Patents (https://lva-virginia.libguides.com/land-grants).
14. Kingsbury, *Vol. 3*, 678–679.
15. McIlwaine, *Minutes*, 91, 138–139. Henry Wilson, Thomas Powell, Christopher Barker, and William Munns were among Captain John Ward's servants who were rescued.
16. Kingsbury, *Vol. 3*, 656–657. [Some spelling was modernized] Using the calculation of 140 acres of land as noted about under the subheading"Company Land or Wilcocks's Plantation?" minus Wilcocks's twenty acres, the estimated number of men that Yeardley may have left at Ackomack is 30.
17. Smith, *Generall Historie*, 302.
18. Kingsbury, *Vol 4*, 11–12.
19. Kingsbury, *Vol. 4*, 67.
20. Kingsbury, *Vol. 4*, 73–74.

Acknowledgments

The records at Eastville are unbroken, reaching into the first twenty-five years of English America. Even Jamestown cannot claim such distinction. Eastville's records, known for their antiquity, are studied by scholars and probed by genealogists. For devotees of history, particularly Virginia history, opening that first book is a life-changing experience. The archaic strokes in age-browned ink are difficult to read but mesmerizing in their graceful loops and curves. Today's writer has the benefit of the work of several transcriptionists—Dr. Susie Ames, Dr. Howard Mackey, Frank Walczyk, and Gail Walczyk. We also have the benefit of the unequaled work of Ralph T. Whitelaw and Anne Floyd Upshur. The accomplishments of these transcriptionists and historians are incomparable gifts to us all.

The Northampton court records are under the care of the office of the Northampton Clerk of the Circuit Court. The clerk and deputies in this office have been invaluable resources for this work. Their dedication as conservators of the records is exemplary and their willingness to assist is more than noteworthy. My sincere thanks to them.

The first of my many steps was taken in the History Room of Eastern Shore Public Library. Thank you to the library staff for their assistance and for their excellent work in garnering one of the best local history collections available anywhere.

I lived in this work for enough years that I have come to feel that I know some of the seventeenth century people better than I know friends and family in the present. Thank you to my friends and family who embraced (and/or tolerated) this trait. For those of you who had the courage to ask, "How's the book?" and the fortitude to endure the answer, my sincere thanks and admiration. For those of you who didn't want a rambling exposition on topics such as "What did George Yeardley contribute to Eastern Shore history?" my sincere thanks and admiration to you as well, because many is the time that I need to stay in the present.

In my family, we are blessed with numerous cousins. Family reunions are a medley of talents, but we rarely have the time or opportunity to know one another beyond the recipes for our covered dishes. I am so fortunate that one of my dear cousins reached out to offer his English expertise as I was shaping an earlier, larger volume of research into written form. Doug Quelch is a man of many talents, interests, and obligations; I am fortunate for his wisdom and his skill. He is a godsend. (Doug would want me to capitalize that word, and in this case, I'd agree as he is God sent.) Doug, thank you for taking each chapter and reading it so carefully. I loved the process and I loved how our cousin relationship has flourished into a true friendship. Now, reader, that being said, what is written in this book is based on the larger volume that Doug read, so any mistakes or quirks of grammar are all my own.

Thank you to readers Dean Sakach, Dawn Conrad, Carolyn Hutchinson, Dr. David Scott, and Carla Shaarda who all read the earlier and larger resource volume. I am grateful for your kind encouragement and your invaluable, insightful suggestions. Thank you to reader Nancy Smith who carefully combed through the current version before I finally let it go for publishing. The careful and reassuring guidance that I have received from my publisher and editor, Kim Eley at KWE Publishing has been a learning endeavor as well as a joyful experience. KWE's Taylor Mills is a gem for her book development skills and patience. Thank you to my sister, Janice Thompson, who has read practically every word I've ever written, always with her favorite pen in hand to neatly note corrections and suggestions. I know that in these years of her first grandchild, reading for me was a true task, especially when he, Ryder, had just discovered that she is a very special person.

Lastly, thank you to the reader. Nothing has been more motivating than to imagine the reader who yearns to hear an untold story or realize a new perspective regarding the spirited and fascinating history of Virginia's Eastern Shore. I pray at least a bit of that is found here.

About the Author

Jenean Hall has relished stories of Virginia history since the days of 4th grade when she and all her classmates were required to make scrapbooks for history class. Reared in a railroad family in a railroad town, Jenean captured memories of that town, Victoria, in her book, *Victoria Stories: Glimpses of a Virginian Railway Town* (2011). During her career as a school psychologist, Jenean moved to Virginia's Eastern Shore, the setting of her maternal grandmother's beloved childhood memories. On weekends and vacations, Jenean pursued the documentation of her grandmother's genealogy and discovered that the presence of that family in Accomack and Northampton counties traces solidly into the seventeenth century, one line reaching back to the nine ships of Jamestown's Third Supply in 1609.

Jenean continues to make her home on Virginia's Eastern Shore where she volunteers to research for special projects such as the Virginia Department of Historic Resource's archaeology excavation at Eyreville Plantation and Northampton Historic Preservation Society's genealogy and history lectures. Her current project is a second book of Eastern Shore history, this one titled *Another Day: More Stories from the Early English Records of Virginia's Eastern Shore*.

www.ingramcontent.com/pod-product-compliance
Lightning Source LLC
Chambersburg PA
CBHW051952290426
44110CB00015B/2205